Praise for Reclaiming the Wild Soul

"*Reclaiming the Wild Soul* touches on so much that makes us more deeply human. But even more, we are invited into a new way of being human. Mary Reynolds Thompson identifies the most powerful qualities of our Earth's great landscapes. She then magically guides us back into a nearly lost realm where we truly feel that our imagination, our inner lives, and our physical selves are an integral expression of the planet herself. To go to the Earth for guidance, we simultaneously go inward to our deeper self and outward to the Great Self of oceans, rivers, deserts, grasslands, mountains, and forests. It is here, as the author writes, 'we learn to live the questions, rather than rush the answers.' *Reclaiming the Wild Soul* reminds us that beyond the flurry and chaos of our cyber-age, there is a primary yet forgotten terrain where we may seek guidance, healing, and wisdom. In doing so, we retrieve our wilder, deeper selves. I read this book with a sense of gratitude. It is a beautiful, passionate, and trustworthy handbook for deeper transformation."

–Lauren de Boer, Executive Editor, *EarthLight,* a magazine of ecology, cosmology, and spirituality.

"Mary Reynolds Thompson's book works simple magic to bind our broken souls back into full-round rapport with the more-than-human terrain. And as the land restores our sanity, we're empowered to work with new clarity to replenish the many-voiced vitality of the animate earth."

–David Abram, author of *The Spell of the Sensuous*

"*Reclaiming the Wild Soul* leads us on a journey of exploration, through imagery, poetry, story and creative imagination, to connect back to the five archetypal landscapes in Nature, and reconnect to our own inherent Nature."

–Angeles Arrien, author of *The Four Fold Way*

"Mary Reynolds Thompson has written a lyrical and potent field guide to reclaiming the wild soul. Her intimacy with Nature and her longing for the reader to experience such intimacy is the golden thread that weaves through every page. Imagine a world in which all women claimed the forests, mountains, oceans, and deserts within our own psyches. It would surely lead us all True North in our quest for personal and planetary wholeness. In *Reclaiming the Wild Soul*, the forests and mountains, the deserts and the oceans, the rivers and the grasslands find their voice. Once heard, we can never forget what they have to say. May we all follow the summons and embark on such a journey. Mary's field guide lights the way."

—Clare Dakin, Founder, TreeSisters

"With ingenuity and subtlety, Mary Reynolds Thompson guides us in ways both old and new to enter Earth's archetypal wildscapes and allow them to infuse us and make us whole again, fully human. Woven with enchanting stories and wise counsel, *Reclaiming the Wild Soul* lavishly supports us, at this time of global crisis/opportunity, to return, emboldened, to Earth and to our own human wildness."

–Bill Plotkin, author of *Wild Mind: A Field Guide to the Human Psyche*

"With the urgency of Rachel Carson and the lyricism of Terry Tempest Williams, Mary Reynolds Thompson brings startling clarity to the myriad ways the earth's archetypal landscapes mirror our own pain, struggles, resources and triumphs. Simultaneously self-help and a courageous call to action, *Reclaiming the Wild Soul* is a vibrant and necessary addition to the literature on ecopsychology, Gaia consciousness, and the thinking person's interior life."

–Kathleen Adams, Director, Center for Journal Therapy, Inc.;
Editor, *Expressive Writing: Foundations of Practice*

"The future of religion and of the planet's health are both connected integrally with our gaining a new sense of reverence for the Earth. Mary Reynolds Thompson's writing provides a creative, fresh approach to this spiritual task. Through language that connects our inner depths with nature's mysterious and challenging beauty, she invites us to deepen our allegiances to our own true nature, to nature itself, and to the source of both."

–The Rev. Fletcher Harper, Executive Director, GreenFaith

"*Reclaiming the Wild Soul* is a gateway into the great spiritual journey of our time: that of nondual consciousness, also called spiritual ecology. These moving stories and images and poetry of Reynolds Thompson will carry you into a fresh, though ancient, realization: the deserts and forests and mountains are there in the universe, and yet simultaneously, they are vibrantly alive in the depths of our souls."

–Brian Swimme, author of *The Hidden Heart of the Cosmos* and co-author (with Thomas Berry) of *The Universe Story*.

"*Reclaiming the Wild Soul* is a must read for anyone on a joyous path to wholeness. Mary Reynolds Thompson's superb book takes us back to our deep roots in nature where our dreams and destiny intertwine. Her book ignites the soul with the earth's powerful wisdom and connects each of us to our deepest, wildest, wisest selves."

–Terry Laszlo-Gopadze, editor of *The Spirit of a Woman*

"What an elegant concept for a book—to engage the reader in the process of surrender, to the light, the texture, the inward quality of the landscape. This is what real writing is—an extended active imagination, a dialogue with our surroundings. It is as much about opening and surrender as it is about craft. It comes down to this: If we can't be captured by world, find our home in it, acknowledge that we are of it, that our minds have been produced by it, then what have we to say that really matters? This book will guide you back to that connection—where the inner world and the outer world meet and simultaneously enrich each other. Reynolds Thompson provides a graceful initiation into an I /Thou relation with the Earth. She is someone I'd like to walk with, into the Dark Wood."

–Valerie Andrews, author of *A Passion for this Earth*.

"Mary Reynolds Thompson asks simple yet profound questions in exploring our connection with nature, and helping us reclaim our wild soul. And reclaim that soul, we must, if we are to find a way towards an Earth that can sustain itself in the face of human consumption and population. She writes in a way that makes you care about this planet, see its beauty on deep levels, and revel in precious moments of discovery and mystery."

-Stephen Altschuler, author of *The Mindful Hiker*

Reclaiming
the Wild Soul

Mary Reynolds Thompson

Foreword by Lorraine Anderson

Reclaiming the Wild Soul

How Earth's Landscapes Restore Us to Wholeness

Wild Roots
PRESS

First edition published 2014, White Cloud Press
Second edition published 2019, Wild Roots Press
Website: www.maryreynoldsthompson.com

Cover and Interior Design by C Book Services
Cover images from pixoto.com
Illustrations by Sophie Brudenell-Bruce—www.sophiebb.com

First Edition: 2014
Second Edition: 2019

Printed in the United States of America

Library of Congress Cataloging-in-Publication Data

Thompson, Mary Reynolds, 1956-
Reclaiming the wild soul : how earth's landscapes restore us to wholeness / Mary
Reynolds Thompson ; foreword by Lorraine Anderson.
pages cm
Includes bibliographical references and index.
ISBN: 978-0-9828894-0-4 (paperback)
978-0-9828894-4-2 (ebook)
1. Human ecology--Philosophy. 2. Landscapes. 3. Nature. 4. Self-realization.
I. Title.
GF21.T48 2014
304.2--dc23
2014027698

For my husband, Bruce, and my mother, Barbara—I dedicate
this book to you with all my wild heart.

In Praise of the Wild Soul

Praise the wild soul for its ridges and canyons, for its rivers and rapids. For its love of deep caves and dark woods. For terrain, vast and varied, undulating beneath spirit sky.

Praise the wild soul for its beauty, tremulous as aspen leaf, fierce as mother hawk. For the way it shuns cages and breaks chains that bind. For the way it rises, wings unfurled, on rhythms of air. No stage holds dancers more graceful than this.

Praise the wild soul for its intricacies, more layered than the beaver's dam, more complex than the termites' hill. Praise its wholeness, no part left out, everything belonging.

Darkness gathers. My heart fills with foreboding at our human frailties.

But I have faith.

I am telling you now:

I believe in the wild soul.

Praise it.

Contents

Foreword

I spent my childhood on a one-acre chicken ranch in the Santa Clara Valley of California, in the days when it was still known as the Valley of Heart's Delight. My three siblings and I grew up climbing trees, catching tadpoles, tromping down the tall grasses to make rooms we played in. In springtime, blossoming orchards stretched as far as the eye could see. The first nine summers of my life, we camped in Cedar Grove, now part of Kings Canyon National Park. I remember the scent of incense cedar in the sunshine, clear blue skies above towering trees, the roaring of rivers, thunderstorms that turned the campground roads into torrents.

Later we moved to north Lake Tahoe, and I would wake at 5:30 and walk out to the main highway through a pine forest newly carved by asphalt roads and fake Swiss chalets. Waiting for the yellow school bus that would take me to the nearest high school, an hour away in Reno, Nevada, I would gaze out over the lake as a chill wind froze my ears. It was always a different shade of blue, some days wind whipped and other days mirror still, and as I breathed it in through my eyes, I felt my heart becoming deep and wild like the lake. During my years attending college in Salt Lake City, I first experienced waking up in a sleeping bag in the red rock desert of southern Utah, trekking to touch wind-carved sandstone arches; it became my sacred ground.

Mary Reynolds Thompson would call this my wild soul story. Her brave and original book has helped me understand that these landscapes—desert, forest, river, mountain, grassland—are woven into the core of my being. It's true that my wild soul has prompted and pushed me to resist cooperating with a culture that worships profit, speed, and efficiency above the beauty and health of the natural world. How to honor my wild soul while making my way in this world has been a central conundrum, as it has been for Thompson, as it may be for you. I began collecting women's writing about nature and eventually left behind a life of editing computer reference manuals in Silicon Valley. In my mid-fifties I found my way to the broad and fertile Willamette Valley of Oregon, where my life has become lush and fruitful.

How do you honor your own wild soul? Picking up this book is a good starting place. Mary Reynolds Thompson understands more clearly than anyone else I know that just as the plants and the animals, the weather and the seasons have their own counterparts in aspects of our being, the landscapes of Earth speak to us. *Reclaiming the Wild Soul* tells us how we can begin to hear them and why it matters. I agree with her that at this time when "every part of Earth is under siege," turning toward a saner way of life must start in the soul of each of us. "The awareness of our oneness with the natural world . . . must become the guiding principle of our life and times," Thompson writes.

And she should know. Tutored by the wild places of Earth—by kayaking the thunderous rapids of the Klamath River, standing on the summit of Mount Shasta ecstatic and terrified as a thunderstorm hits, walking through the Badlands of South Dakota in blinding heat, facing a young bobcat on a neighborhood trail through grasslands— Thompson understands that the pace and hyperrationality of our lives just as much as fracking and mountaintop removal mining are profound insults to the Earth's integrity and our own. She understands how a desert can model spaciousness and simplicity, how we might find ourselves lost in a forest of unknowing in our lives, what rivers and oceans can tell us about flow, how mountains can inspire us to climb toward our passions and purposes, what a grassland can teach us about giving back.

The journey of soul recovery you are about to undertake is of the utmost importance. The hour is late and the stakes are high. For as Thompson writes, "If we don't reclaim and come to love our inner wildness, how much more of the Earth's wild places will we be willing to destroy?" Let the "great rewilding of our world" begin with you, with your pen and your journal and your willingness to slow down, step outside, and let yourself be "absorbed into something larger and less tame" than your small and isolated self.

Lorraine Anderson

Preface

My Own Wild Soul Story

Tell me the landscape in which you live,
and I will tell you who you are.

—José Ortega y Gasset

I believe we each have a wild soul story to tell: an experience in nature that has helped shape who we are and how we live. My own story has its roots in a special place in Italy I visited as a little girl. Trying to imagine my life without Positano is like trying to imagine my life without my parents, or the house I grew up in. It is impossible. You could say Positano is the place where this book began, all those many years ago. You could say it is where all my stories begin.

The moon glinting off water, flying fish leaping from silver surf, and a beach of pebbled stones harboring sea glass smoothed by waves and glowing like jewels. A pig called Romana I rode over mountain trails.

London was where I grew up, but it was the colorful village of Positano on the Amalfi coastline in southern Italy that introduced me to my wild soul.

It was here on holiday as a very young child that I learned to cherish mountains and water, cobblestone streets sticky with the sweetness of grapevines. Sages say there is a line inscribed in our souls for all of our life; if so, that line was written in me by Positano.

The place reached deep into my being. It gifted me with dreams and visions, the wild breath of sea and mountains, the emerald green of grottos. Positano was as different as possible from my orderly life of nannies and nap times, and later, convent boarding school bells and starched uniforms.

I loved it fiercely and passionately.

Language and landscape became the two currents that would shape my life. The first I initially followed down a predictable path: a degree in literature, then copywriting and marketing. Like many, I learned to tame and tailor my nature to suit the requirements of the man-made world. But the manicured lawn didn't suffice for long. A hole grew inside me. I began to drink heavily, seeking aliveness in secretive and unhealthy ways—my life lived in shadow.

I'm not in hiding anymore. I feel like the woman in Clarice Short's poem "The Old One and the Wind" who stands at the edge of the known world welcoming in the elements like a cherished friend.[1] My own path back to the wild soul led me deep into the Earth's great landscapes. For the past thirty years, these wild places have been close companions.

I have trekked the Himalayas, rafted rapids on the Klamath, back-packed the Grand Tetons, drifted down the Irrawaddy River in Burma. Enduring the blasting heat of the Badlands and the freezing winds of Patagonia, gradually I was absorbed into something larger and less tame than my small and isolated self.

Later, language also began to unravel from the tight and predictable. I left marketing and studied to be a facilitator of poetry therapy, exploring poems as if traveling an unknown trail. Lines of poetry stalked me, just as the images of Positano—villas colored like sugar almonds; fishing boats bright as crayons—remained indelibly etched in the geography of my heart.

Nature poetry became my passion. But beyond the poetry of the page, I came to realize that the natural world is itself the greatest poem. Earth's imagery and metaphors speak in powerful ways: they have shown me how to flourish and become whole.

Today, I work with people who are reaching, as if for a foothold, for something more real and more vital than a world of concrete and plastic can provide. I am writing this book for them, for all of us who long to throw open the windows and the doors and let the wild soul in.

The same forces that created Earth created us. We are so much more magnificent than we imagine.

The light in Positano was gentle, golden. It entered my body as a child. Today, the same rich golden light greets me every day in Northern California, where I make my home. When my life became small and dark and I was forced to confront my addiction, I realized that the light was inside me still—it had never gone out. It was there to illuminate my way forward. It is the same light that reminds me that life is a wild adventure, filled with sacredness and wonder.

I know the pain of being tamed, of being ripped from the roots and fashioned to fit the narrow purview of our modern world. Yet inner and outer nature evolve together. We are part of this amazing world we inhabit; her creativity and her power are our birthright.

To feel the breath of wildness come into your body is to reclaim your natural wholeness. It is to be enfolded by fields of grasses and held by the mountains' slow and steady strength. It is to hear in your own heartbeat the thunderous roar of the ocean, reminding you that your life still belongs to the wild Earth.

All you have to do is reach for her.

Introduction

The Journey of the Soulscapes

Remember the earth whose skin you are . . .

–Joy Harjo

Every spiritual journey is at its heart a quest for wholeness. We long to feel a part of the vast and unfolding mystery of life. We yearn to feel alive, engaged. We are seeking our place and purpose. But how do we proceed? How do we remember who we are? What path will carry us home?

This book maps a journey into the wild environs of the soul through five archetypal landscapes: deserts, forests, oceans and rivers, mountains, and grasslands. I call these "soulscapes," for they are the merging of inner and outer nature—the meeting place of self and Earth. As you enter their depths, you will awaken the metaphors of the landscapes within you and lay claim to the wild wisdom and power at the core of your being.

Humans, after all, weren't placed on Earth; we emerged out of the Earth. Every day, we consume part of the Earth in order to stay alive. The great landscapes of the planet are our ancestors; they arose from the Earth just as we did, and their energies evoke deep feelings and potentialities within us at both conscious and unconscious levels.

Since the remarkable appearance of self-reflective consciousness around 200,000 years ago, we have been primed to connect with these regions—they are resident in our collective unconscious, part of our primal birth matrix. The cultural historian Thomas Berry puts it this way in *Dream of the Earth*: "Beyond our genetic coding, we need to go to the earth, as the source whence we came, and ask for her guidance, for the earth carries the psychic structure as well as the physical form of every living being upon the planet."[1]

Today, as concern grows about how far we have distanced ourselves from the natural world, we are encouraged to spend more time outdoors, walking, gardening, or simply being in nature. These things are hugely important. But this book asks something more: it invites you to awaken to the ancient Earth-consciousness that resides within you—within us all—that you can access at any time, in any place, even in the midst of the busiest city.

The landscapes you will explore in this book are not external or extrinsic to who you are; they are woven into the core of your being as surely as elements from the stars or the salty depths of the oceans. For this is the amazing truth: four billion years of Earth wisdom are embedded in your cells. It is time to awaken to the whole magnificent geography of your soul.

The Wounded Wild

You may be understandably keen to get started down your personal path, but it is important to take a moment to grasp the relationship between your inner nature and the natural world. For it is this relationship that lies at the heart of the journey we will take together in this book.

When we consider how embedded we are in the Earth, how we are literally made of the same stuff as rivers, rocks, and roots, we can see how separating from this beautiful, fecund world might be damaging to our psyches. Have you ever suffered a terrible accident, betrayal, or loss? Then you know you can be left depleted, depressed, perhaps even cast adrift. It is as if some part of your soul leaves you. As if you aren't quite whole.

In losing our intimate relationship with the Earth, we modern humans have suffered a particular trauma that has caused our wild souls to split off. We may not always be fully aware of what is happening, so accustomed have we become to our high-speed, high-tech, built-up lives. Yet even if we remain unconscious of the source of our pain, we experience the symptoms of separation in a sense of alienation and a lack of aliveness.

Modernity, with its mechanistic mind-set, excels at certain things: expediency, efficiency, uniformity. But the wild soul—who you really are—gets its sense of power and imagination from the natural world, and thrives on an altogether different set of values: creativity, authenticity, diversity. Exiled from Earth, like a wounded animal the wild soul goes into hiding. And we are left feeling off balance and incomplete.

Our psyches then look for any available means to experience a sense of wild freedom. Addiction, to everything from alcohol and shopping to technology and pharmaceutical mood enhancers, is a frequent symptom of the soul's desire to break free of the deadening aspects of modernity. This default approach—what I term living the "shadow wild"—only takes us further from our source. In the end, we find ourselves trapped, tamed, and unfulfilled.

So how do we heal the wounded wild? How do we reclaim our wild souls? The answer lies within each of us.

Are you able to recall a moment when as a child you lay in the branches of a tree, or idled the day away watching clouds dance by? Do you remember how alive your senses were? How peaceful or full of possibilities you felt? How the Earth held and supported you?

Even now, something as simple as the gentle brush of a breeze or the sight of a beautiful sunset can remind you that, beyond the confines of your everyday reality, Earth is calling to you. It holds wisdom for your life and points toward something vaster and more vibrant within you. There is something fierce, free, and genuine that longs to find expression through your one particular and wild life.

But these moments pass too quickly. Subsumed back into our hyperrational, fast-paced existences, our sense of interconnectedness becomes, like so many holiday snapshots, a pleasant but ineffective memory.

The awareness of our oneness with the natural world can no longer be allowed to recede into the background. If we are to ensure a vibrant future not only for ourselves but for the entire Earth community, it must become the guiding principle of our life and times. At this precise moment in human history, it is vital that we bridge the false divide between the human and nonhuman worlds lest we risk losing the wild beauty that is our deepest nature and greatest hope.

Reclaiming our identity as part of the wild and evolving Earth is both the journey and the ultimate purpose of this book. This is what the human soul longs for: to become itself a force of nature by liberating its instinctive, creative expression through each of us. In this way lies wholeness.

In the following sections, I'll lay out the essential foundation for the journey we are about to embark upon—explaining how we arrived at this point and providing a map of where we are going and how we can navigate the terrain. But first a question: how did this split between Earth and self come about, and what does it tell us about our own journey?

How We Got Here

For many hundreds of generations, humanity's primary relationship was with the Earth. Our ancestors engaged with the land, the water, and the creatures around them in a direct and intimate way. Looking skyward at the night stars, they told stories of their place in the great scheme of things. Life was hard, brutally so at times, but they never questioned their sense of belonging to a community of life with which they were inextricably entwined.

About 10,000 years ago, we began the transformation from hunter-gatherers to agriculturalists, thus shifting our primary social form of organization. Increasingly adept at cultivating the soil and no longer nomadic, we settled down and began to build civilizations; sprawling cities gave rise to progressively more complex political structures, art, music, and drama. As language migrated from the spoken to the written word, we began to seek wisdom in books rather than in the shifting constellations, the rustle of a tree branch, the paw print on the path.

In the seventeenth century, with its heightened emphasis on reason, intellect, and science, Earth came to be viewed not as a source of spiritual nurture and wisdom but as a resource. Perceiving ourselves as separate from and superior to the Earth, neither restrained by her laws nor beholden to her bounty, we began to exploit the planet in ever more devastating ways. And our Western religious practices support-ed us in doing so. What was sacred was no longer sought in the great spread of prairies, forests, and oceans, but relegated to an unearthly realm called Paradise.

Even so, throughout the nineteenth century and during the initial years of the twentieth, we still lived in a largely wild world. There were still places teeming with wildlife and devoid of human settlement. Oceans still churned with large fish and remained empty of plastic. Large rivers still ran free in the main, and thick pelts of forests covered vast swathes of the planet. Most humans still lived close to the land rather than in cities, as they had done for all of human history.

Our current century presents a very different picture. Rivers and prairies, mountaintops and oceans—every part of Earth is under siege. Unspoiled, wild nature is disappearing all around us. It becomes harder and harder to feel a part of what Gary Snyder calls "the whole mountains-and-rivers mandala universe."[2] While it is vital that we acknowledge the grief of this loss, becoming paralyzed by pain serves neither us nor the greater world.

It's easy to be overwhelmed by the challenges that confront us. But what if the process of rewilding the Earth began with rewilding our souls? If we truly grasp the interconnectedness between all living things, doesn't it follow that every change within us will be reflected in the whole? If we reroot ourselves in the rhythms, wisdom, and patterns that created this planet and our own flesh and feelings, what might be possible for the Earth and all her inhabitants? What if healing the world really does start from within?

And so we begin by taking a journey deep into the heart of the soulscapes.

Following the path inward, we enter the stillness of deserts, the mystery of forests, the flow of rivers and oceans, the strength of moun-tains, and the vast openness of grasslands that reside within us. In so doing, we uncover a truth that has the power to change the way we live, act, and dream: when we awaken to our oneness with the Earth, we tap

Wild Soul Wisdom Model

In our journey through the soulscapes, we evolve. We transform from the small egocentric self, separate from the Earth and other beings, to the wilder and more encompassing ecocentric self, an integral part of an ensouled planet.

MODERN WORLDVIEW Egocentric ⟶	WILD SOUL WISDOM ⟶ ⟶ Ecocentric
Belief: Separation We are separate from the earth. What happens to the earth—and how we treat it—have no bearing on our own psyches and souls.	**Belief: Wholeness** Our consciousness is part of the greater body and intelligence of Earth herself. Whatever we do to the Earth, we do to ourselves.
Experience: Alienation We are estranged from the earth. We experience an inner loneliness, a sense that we are not enough, however much we achieve or acquire. We are disconnected from our bodies and emotions.	**Experience: Belonging** We belong to a sacred planet where everything holds meaning and significance. We are vibrantly alive, connected, part of the greater community of life. We are rooted in a sense of place and purpose.
Being: Domesticated We deny our instinctual and primal selves, exalting the security of the human-built world over nature and the spontaneity of life. Our behaviors are often predictable and mechanistic.	**Being: Wild** We are sensual, instinctive, and intuitive beings. We favor inquisitiveness over acquisitiveness. We source our creativity, wisdom, and aliveness from the natural world.
Affirmation: I renounce the worldview of separation, alienation, and domestication.	**Affirmation:** I embrace the wisdom of wholeness, belonging, and wildness.

into a wealth of resources and wisdom that enable us to live fully and passionately, as cocreators in the great and evolving story of this planet.

In reclaiming our wild souls, we discover a way for all of life to flourish and thrive, ourselves included.

Finding Our Way Back Home

When I first began to live in a way that honored my own wild soul, I felt removed from friends and family. I was like a lone king penguin I once encountered on Gable Island, off the tip of Tierra del Fuego.

He stood very still on a pebbly beach beside the Beagle Channel, his round black eyes set off by yolk-yellow markings and his body covered in a scrubby set of feathers. Cut off from his community because his new feathers were still in the process of growing in, he couldn't yet brave the icy waters; he hadn't the proper insulation. As the new feathers thrust through his skin, I would later learn, they caused him pain.

Transformation is rarely easy. At times, you may long to retreat to a less vital and more domesticated vision of yourself. But remember: the strength of the Earth resides within you, supporting you in your quest for wholeness.

This became very clear to me in a dream I had when I first began to write this book.

> *I am floating miles above the planet, looking down at what appear to be ants emerging from the Earth's fiery core. Drifting closer, I realize they are women. They stream out from the center of the Earth to encircle the globe, pounding tall sticks, beating a rhythmic pulse, straight-backed, sinewy. Closing ranks around the Earth, they form a protective circle of love and healing. They are fierce warriors, strong beyond belief.*

These women represent all of us who are in touch with our wild souls. They illustrate the strength that comes when we claim the "I am-ness" of a mountain or a forest. In owning our birthright as beings of the Earth, we emerge as purposeful, passionate, filled with molten power.

Whether you're drawn to take this journey because you want to throw off the constraints of modernity, or you're a dedicated Earth lover and long to be supported in your efforts to make the world a better place, or you simply yearn for a wildness that brings you more creativity, freedom, and bravery—regardless of your starting point, this journey will carry you home.

In your willingness to pick up this book, you have already taken a step toward embracing a more passionate and fully realized existence. My belief is that you can already glimpse your wild soul returning.

Navigating the Journey

This is a guidebook to your wild soul, and I encourage you to pick it up and refer to it often. Once you become oriented to the five landscapes, either by reading straight through the book or by reading the short descriptions of the soulscapes later in this introduction, you can enter the journey at any place you choose.

You might begin by asking, "Which soulscape am I in right now?" Life propels you toward certain aspects of the soul, but you can also intuit where you need to go and which soulscapes to embrace at any given time. As a weary traveler in the desert, you might choose to head to the oceans and rivers to reclaim your balance and flow. Or you may find yourself too far out of your comfort zone in the mountains and feel the need to return to the mystery and wisdom of the forests.

It takes courage to enter the natural wilderness, and to willingly enter the vast terrain of our souls. Some of the teachings found in these landscapes come in the form of challenges, calling forth a hidden strength or demanding we confront our shadow. As a recovering alcoholic, now thirty years sober, I was once terrified of the desert. I wanted nothing to do with it. Addicted to excess and riddled with dark secrets, I found the bright light of the desert—and its chronic dryness—exposing and cruel. Learning to make friends with the solitude and silence of the desert was hugely important in healing the inner wound that led to my addiction.

In a similar way, you, too, may find yourself attracted to certain landscapes, leery of others. In your quest for wholeness, however, you will in time learn to embrace them all.

Taken together, the soulscapes form the arc of a heroic journey in which you set off on your quest by leaving behind community to enter the great silence of the deserts, discover ancient wisdom in the forests, plunge into the depths of your longings in the oceans and rivers, confront personal challenges in the mountains, and return to community in the grasslands.

What follow are brief descriptions of the stages of the journey.

Deserts

We come to the desert to transform. Here, winds named khamsin, sirocco, and simoom make and remake the land, leaving it unrecognizable, surprising. And here, too, death and disappointment reshape our inner landscape, inviting something new to be born within. As we make our pilgrimage to this expansive, silent place, we lay bare the bones of our being, and in doing so uncover deep wells of inner awareness and strength.

Forests

What will emerge from the shadows? What is stalking us? What longs to break through? In the dark forest, far from comforting signposts, we learn to live in mystery. We are less certain, but we are more alive. Between light and shadow, Earth and sky, we walk the pathless path, discovering our unique creativity, wisdom, and sense of timing. We awaken to a deeper sense of self.

Oceans and Rivers

The waters of the world shape the topography of the Earth; the flow of our longings gives direction to our lives. As we learn to move from the shallow waters of superficial desire, we discover the emotional vitality that comes when we live from the pure depths of our being. But not before we learn to navigate the many forms that longing can take—some destructive, some life-giving.

Mountains

Mountains speak to the power within us to shape our world according to what we truly value. Without mountains the Earth would flatten into endless monotony. Without the need to aspire to great heights, our lives would be equally dull. When we seek our full aliveness, we scale the mountains to lay claim to our own granite and grandeur. Filled with risks, challenges, and even setbacks and sacrifices, the mountains give our lives a heroic edge.

Grasslands

In the grasslands, rivers slow to steady streams, herds of antelope and other creatures gather to drink from the waters, and homesteaders declare their long journey over and put down roots. A wide expanse of grassland is like an invitation to settle down, create community, celebrate, and offer thanks. In cherishing our place in the world, we learn to build relationship with all our neighbors—and not just the human variety.

In my work as a facilitator of poetry therapy, I have guided hundreds of people through these five landscapes and have been privileged to hear many stories, some of which I will share with you in the following pages. To protect the confidentiality of those who wish to remain anonymous, I have changed names and sometimes identifying characteristics such as gender or job. The stories, however, remain a true reflection of what was shared. Where people are happy to be known, you'll find their names listed in the acknowledgments section.

I promise that you will also experience many moments of insight along the way—some subtle and others miraculous. The natural metaphors that emerge from these regions penetrate deep into the soul. The more you work with them, the more their power will be transferred to you. The flow of rivers, the solidity of mountains, the resilience of the grasslands will come alive in your own depths, shifting your perceptions and behaviors at a bedrock level.

I have focused on the qualities that most often emerge when I work with others, and that have spoken forcibly to me. You, however, will discover metaphors and messages of your own. These landscapes have the capacity to shape our sensibilities and speak to us in many tongues. I know this firsthand.

In beginning this book, I had a fixed idea that every soulscape would have six qualities, each of which would fit into about three pages and take a certain form. The Earth must have laughed at my attempt to wrap up her wild wisdom in neat little packages! My rational, planned approach didn't work. Ahead, you'll find different voices and tones, short and long pieces. In surrendering to the landscapes, I had to give up control. Such is the way of writing from the wild soul! And living from it too.

Give yourself fully to this journey, and the landscapes will likewise work on you. The goal is therefore not to merely identify or "visit" your inner wildness, but to express it fully and vibrantly in the way that you live. I ask that you take the time to slow down: listen to the river's song, root yourself in tree wisdom, inhabit the sturdiness of rock. To be in relationship with the Earth, you must take the time to know her.

The explorations that follow each chapter will give you ways to intensify and enrich your journey. They are designed to help you develop a listening spirit and deeper intimacy with the world around you. I've also included brief reflective writing exercises to help you integrate your insights, an essential part of your transformational process. In order to get the most out of your journey, I suggest you keep a special journal to record your experiences.

A brief note about language usage: Today many choose to lowercase the "e" in "Earth." Environmentalist Bill McKibben has gone so far as to title one of his books *Eaarth* to draw attention to how greatly we humans have altered our home planet. I prefer "Earth," straight up and capitalized, because it honors our place in the Universe, which, as you can see, I also choose to capitalize. Regarding plants and other living creatures, I have chosen to use the pronouns "him" or "her." Whenever we refer to a member of the nonhuman world as "it," we further objectify and distance ourselves from our Earth community. If any of these preferences—or seeming inconsistencies—confuse you, please understand that they make sacred sense to this author, as I trust they will to many readers too.

This is a wild and sacred journey. There is no wrong place to go. No wrong turn to take. For you are not headed in any preordained direction; you are not expected to become anything other than who you already are. As you dwell among these pages, traveling from landscape to landscape, paying attention to the outside terrain and the wildness within you, this I know: you will discover that who you are already is so much greater than you ever dreamed.

And beneath your feet, the nurturing Earth will hold you up, guiding you to reclaim the rich diversity and lushness of your own wild soul.

THE WILD SOUL AFFIRMATION MANDALA

As you move outward from the affirmations at the center of the mandala, you are deepening your sense of oneness with the Earth and her powerful landscapes. Say each affirmation out loud and allow your body to receive the wisdom that each one offers you.

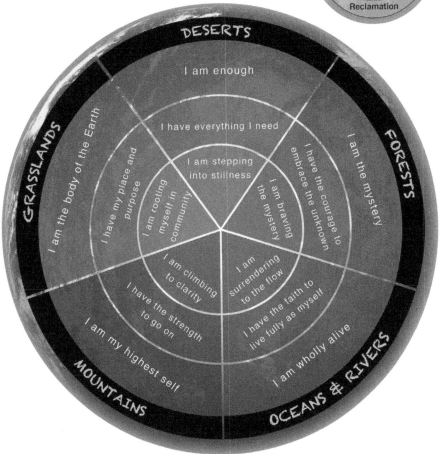

PART 1
Deserts

*I will speak to you in desert language,
answer with a lizard's tongue.*

The rhythm of day is the rhythm of fire . . .
–Jay Griffiths

More than one-fifth of the Earth's surface is desert. The largest desert of all, the Sahara, sweeps across Africa covering an expanse the size of the United States. Deserts come in many forms: the red rocks of Utah; the painted deserts of Arizona; the great gravel plains of the Gobi; the Sonora, with its forest of cacti; the vast expanses of the Kalahari and the Mojave—the hottest, driest places on the planet.

We experience the desert in many ways. In winds named khamsin, sirocco, and simoon that shape and reshape the terrain, making and remaking the land. In the cracks and creases of our skin, in the thirst on our tongues, in the dry fear that catches at our throats, in the loneliness that grips us amid a busy street or bustling day, in the dust rising to meet us at the end of the road.

We carry the desert within us in our timeless terror of snakes. We carry it in Bible stories, Psalms, in the songlines of the Australian aborigines, in our own longing for the silence, simplicity, and spaciousness so at odds with the crowded complexity of contemporary life. In artist Georgia O Keeffe's bleached bones and sensual desert blooms.

Whether you have spent time in an actual desert or not, the mere mention of "desert" conjures up images, feelings, and sensations that are part of your own wild soul. The desert occupies a significant, though often infrequently visited, region within us.

For some, the desert is an inviting landscape, for others a more challenging one. When I once presented the soulscapes to a group of women writers, one responded, "I hate the desert. I'm not going there." Perhaps you, too, feel that way. If so, I suggest you simply becoming curious—what is it about the desert that frightens or repels you? This is part of your journey of self-discovery, and you may be surprised by the answers you find.

My friend Kim was at a silent retreat when she awoke one morning to a sense of acute emptiness and aching loneliness. When asked later by her Rinpoche, her Buddhist teacher, what that emptiness felt like, she immediately responded, "The desert."

"Then spend time contemplating the desert," her teacher told her.

At first Kim saw only "nothingness" in the desert soulscape. Then, slowly, she began to notice the different colors of the sands, the tiny plants, the flick of the lizard's tail and other often quite lovely life forms. At the same time she realized that her sense of aloneness had likewise been an illusion. Her inner emptiness turned out to be filled with delightful nuance and subtle forms of life.

Her relationship to both her loneliness and the desert landscape were transformed. She later told me, with a huge grin, "I don't fear either anymore. They are both precious to me."

Another woman shared with me that she knew in her heart she was a desert dweller. Her life had been arduous from the day she was born. As a young woman she'd signed up for the military and spent time in the deserts of Saudi Arabia. Life hadn't gotten easier. She said this: "I know how to bloom wherever I am planted. Life's been hard, but I've learned to live fully even so." I could feel her strength and realness as something powerful, beautiful, and strong—like a prickly cactus that holds healing salve at her center.

As the desert landscape shifts and changes, so the reasons we find ourselves in the desert soulscape may differ according to our circumstances. We may be propelled to the desert in search of time and space to think. Or perhaps we are reluctant visitors, brought to this bleached-bone terrain by the death of a loved one or another profound loss of some kind. We may find ourselves in a literal dry spell that parches our creativity and covers our lives with a dull dust of fatigue.

Time in the desert soulscape will reveal to us who we are and what we really want. In one sense we might even say that the desert—a place far removed from community and the busyness of everyday life—is the region where all heroic journeys begin.

CHAPTER 1
Silence

*Your old life was a frantic running
from silence.*

–Jelal al-Din Rumi

No bird or water song. No rustle of leaves or barking of dogs, just miles of parched earth and shifting sand dunes. In the vast world of the desert, the movements of snake and scorpion sound like the crack of a snare drum. The slightest shift in wind is noticeable. Silence carves out space inside of us, empties us.

In the desert, sound waves that would pulse long and far on moist air weaken. Sound is muffled, stopped in its tracks just as we are by the fiery heat—the dust-dry atmosphere.

Listen. Can you hear the breath of your own existence?

I went to the desert as I began this book. I needed to hear myself think.

My husband and I rented a small cabin near Joshua Tree National Park in the high desert of Southern California, for a week in December. I'd awake in the chill of the morning, wrap myself in a large quilt, and take a cup of coffee and my journal outside. In the cool of dawn, the quail bustled, curve-billed thrashers crocheted the earth with needle-sharp beaks, and tiny, brightly colored birds scuffled on the ground. As the sun rose and the heat intensified, the world quieted.

Midmorning we'd set out into the desert, moving slowly in the heat. We climbed steep, rocky canyons, listening for the brittle thrum of rattlers. We passed Joshua trees, some burned black from fire. We nestled in the cool of caves to eat our lunches.

One night I stood and gazed at a honeycomb of stars, remembering the story of the South African writer Laurens van der Post and the Bushman of the Kalahari—how distraught they were to learn that van der Post couldn't hear the stars singing, and that they treated him like a sick man, so sorry were they for his loss.

I strained to listen.

I thought of how hard it is to find peace and quiet amid the noise and hustle of our hectic lives. How we are so entranced by our marvelous evolutionary gift of language that we often neglect our intuitive, wordless knowing. How technology adds another layer of noise and separation that can keep us from our intuition and the language of the nonhuman world.

"Man who has lost silence has not merely lost one human quality, but his whole structure has been changed thereby, " Max Picard writes in 1948 in *The World of Silence*.[1] That night, the vast, timeless tranquility of the desert reached deep inside me. I was startled to hear the rhythmic beating of my heart.

The desert silence, at first frightening and overwhelming, began to feel essential—welcome. This wasn't the soundlessness of loneliness or loss, but a deep, comforting silence that let in light, beauty, meaning. I learned to sit quietly for minutes at a time, then longer. The soundless expansiveness of the desert seemed to slow, then almost extinguish, all the internal and external chatter. Like the sculpted contours of the rocks around me, this book began to take shape in my mind.

On our last morning, sad to leave but deeply peaceful, I sat quietly on the porch outside our cabin and watched a small cottontail dart between the cacti, halting now and again. Then, in a flash, the rabbit bounded forward and snuggled her twitching nose into my slipper. We looked at each other wide-eyed before she dashed away.

By letting go of my inward chatter, I had invited this shy, vulnerable creature into my sphere. She had gifted me with her trust. If I continued to absorb the desert's gift of silence, what other marvelous things would find me on this journey?

Would I, too, hear the singing of the stars?

Silence Exploration

Spending time in silence each day is an essential step in your journey. Five minutes a day is fine at first, but over the course of a month, see if you can work your way up to twenty minutes, and then even longer. At first you may struggle to quell your inner chatter. Don't fight it; just try to return your mind to your breath, or focus on an object in front of you, or a pleasant sensation like the sun on your face. You can do this exercise sitting quietly at home or outdoors in a special spot. If you prefer, make a practice of walking in silence.

After each period of silence, take out your journal and reflect on these questions:

> What did I notice?
> What did I hear?
> What or who is speaking to me right now?

CHAPTER 2
Thirst

In the desert the most urgent thing is to wait.

–Alessandro Ponzato

When we are dry in our bones, dusty from fatigue, bent double with grief, the desert calls to us. We enter parched and exhausted, every cell of our body, every inch of our being, thirsting for water.

We do not tell our friends what is going on. We do not take phone calls. We neglect our families. Like other desert inhabitants, we learn to adapt, burrow, go dormant.

We grow big ears like the fennec fox to release heat; we gather moisture in our belly like the cactus; dew becomes more precious than pearls. Our skin grows thick and barbed. We move only when necessary, slow our heartbeats.

Some will pronounce us dead.

Invisible, we live underground, cooled by layers of desert sand. Avoid sunlight. Forage under a full moon, padding on paws that cushion us from thorns. Howl like the coyote in the night. Grow a long, curling tongue like the fruit bat to seek out sweetness in the dark. Discover we have the ability of the wildebeest to scent damp earth from miles away.

Parched but patient, our skins dry out, nails splinter, hearts crack.

And when the rain finally arrives, it finds the broken part of us, and enters.

Thirst Exploration

How will you learn to adapt when fatigue or grief grip you?

Imagine you're an inhabitant of the desert during a particularly dry period. Begin your writing with the words "I am the creature who . . . or I am the plant who . . ." Allow your imagination to lead you into your adaptive and survival strategies. Write for ten minutes, or longer if you're comfortable. When you've finished, take a moment to reflect on what you wrote and ask: "What have I learned about waiting out this dry period of my life?"

Take a few more moments to jot down your insights.

CHAPTER 3
Simplicity

A condition of complete simplicity
(Costing not less than everything)

−T. S. Eliot

In the desert, water is a gift. When it arrives the air fills with surprising birdsong and the land erupts in robes of flowers. Escape-pod seeds, dormant for years, await the first generous rains to burst forth and bloom.

And all of this is more beautiful because it is not an everyday event. *What is it you truly need?*

I sit near Balanced Rock in Arches National Park in Utah. The bare shape of the rock and its every crevice are slowly revealed as the sun lifts from behind the horizon. There is no hint in the steely morning air of the heat that will follow.

A thermos of tea, earmuffs, a pad to sit on. In the desert morning, joy grows in my spirit like wildflowers as rocks come alive, take shape, run red. Like blood and gold. Perhaps I can be more present because in the desert the earth is more present—each thing perceived more clearly than in other regions, where contours are masked by vegetation. I am somehow more aware of—more visible to—myself.

Absence of clutter and the capacity to hold something back are what make the desert beautiful. The empty space in a sculpture is as important as, or more important than, the clay or stone that remains. As I sit here, I know that the American Dream as it exists today will not survive the desert. This unquenchable desire for more—for greater things and constant growth—seems to have no place in this unforgiving land. Las Vegas, in the end, will be no match for the Mojave. Over time, the essential desert earth will refuse to sustain it.

This land, after all, is beautiful, but its beauty is precarious. Like a long pause after a bar of music, or a Zen-styled room free of any extraneous object, its grandeur—and its survival—are predicated on restraint.

A student of mine once told me the desert reminded her of a beautiful woman with no makeup or artifice, just fine bones. And I think this is true. Less is more where there is beauty at heart.

What is it that I need?

Simplicity and necessity, the absence of clutter and excess, bring us closer to what is vibrant and alive. The prickly cactus bears life-giving juice at its center. Life without illusions, based on simple needs, can yield tremendous inner riches.

We come to the desert in part because we want to know who we are without all our external paraphernalia. This is a profoundly spiritual way to live: in the lean bone marrow of life. The way light streams upward across a bare rock face like melting gold, nothing standing between it and the simple form of the rock.

All things are eventually illuminated in the desert. The light scours all. There is nowhere to hide.

In the desert we get clear on what truly matters to us—water, food, shelter, love, family, community, meaningful work. The rest blisters and burns away under the relentless heat of day, under nights exploding with stars.

Freed from excess, our lives can begin to mirror the exquisiteness of the night-blooming saguaro. In the dead of dark, with no person to witness it, the cactus unfurls a single, lavish bloom, the bleached bone of moonlight and with the fragrance of musk. Lesser long-nosed bats rise up and seek her out, their long tongues licking up syrup. This is sweetness so miraculous, so rare and astonishing, the bats travel thousands of miles, often leaving their pups, to feed.

This is the way of the desert: beauty that waits, lavishness that is restrained. Moments of exploding sensuality bordered by long stretches of severity that do not detract from life's bounty, but highlight it . . . turn a simple sip of water into a moment of grace.

What is it you truly need?

Simplicity Exploration

Create a desert corner in your home. You might find some interesting rocks, cacti, or a miniature sandbox to decorate. Most important is that this particular area be as uncluttered as possible. The kind of place that feels serene and understated.

If you have children, tell them about this special space. Let them know that any member of the household is welcome to visit, but mustn't leave anything behind. It is to remain mess free. If your home doesn't allow for this, find a space somewhere in your neighborhood where you experience ease and simplicity.

After spending time in your serene space, write your responses to these questions:

What do I notice about my internal terrain when I am in a clutter-free space?

How can I incorporate more simplicity into my life?

What might I need to let go of?

What is it I truly need?

CHAPTER 4
Clarity

One needs time in the desert to see.

–Terry Tempest Williams

Coyote energy is afoot in the desert. The heat shimmers and distorts, bends reality, turns rocks into ravens, trees into towering strangers. Sands ripple like clear pools in the distance. The desire to quench your thirst is real, but the water before you is not.

What you see isn't always what exists.

This is a dreamscape of illusion, magic, and mischief. Phantasmagorical rock formations and restless sands play tricks on your eyes. Haunting images swirl up from hoodoos and drift across eerie moonscapes. A colorful caravan moves across the desert, its tracks disappearing beneath a blasting wind. Things carry less weight here, are less fixed and entrenched. Old beliefs, unexamined assumptions, outmoded worldviews vanish like yesterday's footsteps in the slightest breeze.

Away from a concrete landscape grown hard with certitude, our imaginations are released into a fluid and more magical realm. The air is clear, the view unimpeded by trees and vegetation, all the way to the wide horizon. And yet, for all this clarity, perception is both uncertain and paradoxical. In the desert we see that a dream can lead to truth while a supposed truth, once uncovered, may turn to dust. The ground of our being shifts. In a world that is constantly changing, what is real? What is false?

Home to misfits, mystics, truth tellers, fools, hermits, dreamers, and poets—the desert belongs to those who perceive the world differently. They burrow deep, look beyond neat boxes and limited notions, beyond the social norms that cage our minds and keep us on a narrow track. Grand visions are born here, and they die here too. Everything is suspect, and yet everything is deeply magical.

Survival depends on taking nothing for granted. You learn to become self-reliant, keenly knowledgeable about the terrain. Each thing must be scrutinized. Perhaps gold can be mined here? Or perhaps only fool's gold. It is for you to discover.

One night, camping in the desert, I experienced the power of desert "seeing" in a dream.

A huge snake with a blue collar of glittering stones rises up from the center of a television set, tongue flickering. I am in awe of her majesty and shimmering gold scales. Wordlessly, the snake tells me that I am to translate what I am hearing on a foreign station for others to understand. I am uncertain, but I am not afraid. I know I must obey.

Later, I learned when studying *Medicine Cards,* images based on traditional Native American wisdom, that the snake represents cosmic unity, connection to all things. The snake's medicine is concerned with transmuting a thought, action, or desire so wholeness can be achieved. The glittering blue collar nestled around the throat represents the fifth chakra: the ability to express that wholeness through creativity. The dream was an illusion that taught me about the essence of my calling. This is how the desert helps us see.

There are times when the greatest gift you can give yourself is to give up being "normal" for a while, or trying to conform. Exiled from ordinary, everyday society and activities, in the desert of your soul, away from the world's insistent demands, you learn to navigate the realm of dreams and synchronicities that awaken you to fresh insights. Lines of poetry carve themselves into the canyons of your soul. You are forced to question your perceptions, and you develop acuity—a clarity of vision.

Here, when coyote howls, you answer with your own mischievous song, proclaiming the world as you see it through wild, unprejudiced eyes.

Clarity Exploration

Write down a belief that you have. For example, that you need to stay with your job no matter what, or that nothing really changes, or that you're the only one who knows what's right for a situation you find yourself in. Then choose a quiet spot, settle down, and take a moment to imagine that you are in the desert—better still, actually visit one. As you speak your belief aloud, notice how it feels in your body. How does the air seem to receive your perceived belief? Does your statement feel true? Now get out your journal and write two short pieces.

First: "This belief is *true* because . . ."

Then: This belief is *untrue* because . . ."

As you reflect on your two answers, write a third short reflection:

"This is the perspective that would most serve me and others . . ."

As you describe your "perfect vision" or perspective, invite this new way of seeing into your dreams and daily imagination so it can grow clearer and more real.

CHAPTER 5
Emptiness

But in this nothing we find what we did not know existed.

–Susan Griffin

CRYPTOBIOTICS: KEEP OFF. I was hiking in the Mojave Desert when these words stopped me in my tracks: "Crypto," hidden, "biotics," life. Hidden life. I knelt down and peered at the desert floor. I could just discern the lichens, mosses, and cynobacteria embroidering the soil in delicate stitches and lacework. Nearly invisible, this was a living ground cover that bound the soil and captured moisture—vital, yet so easily destroyed by unmindful footsteps.

Entranced by the fine webbing at my feet, I thought about the people who visit the desert in droves to view the wildflowers each spring, and how few of them stop to admire the hidden life that makes these flowers possible. Beneath the flash and form resides the ground of our being, so essential to our survival.

Yet how often do we trample the hidden life within us? And at what cost?

The desert's resistance to cultivation is an affront to the Western sensibility of what land should be: productive, hardworking, industrious, in other words, all the things we believe give a place—and a person—value. We perceive the desert as *terra nullius*, defining it by what we see as an absence of life.

Yet isn't it true that within you lies a place beyond the reach of cultivation and exploitation? A place that simply is . . . regardless of what you do, whom you love, or how you look. The Bushmen of the Kalahari describe themselves as the desert in human form. Don't you, too, contain such a world?

Our desire to alter and capitalize on our environments can keep us from making peace with our true nature. As long as we're engaged in self-improvement projects, we feel productive, as if we're getting somewhere. But the desert is most itself under a searing sun, when the world stills and the kangaroo rats and spiny toads burrow underground, the lizards hug the scant shade of bushes, and nothing moves. And aren't you, also, most yourself when you become still, empty—even of thought?

Spare and spacious, the desert soulscape invites us into the vast expanse at our center—the great plain of the inner spirit—where we observe, without agenda, what we find there. In this way, the desert supports the development of *witness* consciousness: clear sight, and acceptance of what is seen.

Witness consciousness finds expression in the Australian aboriginal songlines, or dreaming tracks, they use to map their land. An aborigine can travel vast distances over the dry, red-earthed outback, which to our eyes appears monotonous and lifeless. For him, each dip in the ground, each cool shadowed slope, holds a story of water, animals, plants, and ancestors. A songline is the most precious gift an aborigine possesses, because the song maps every aspect of the land, providing detailed and life-saving knowledge.

This kind of witnessing doesn't view the self as separate from the land. It is seeing as celebration, as intimacy, as oneness. It is the Bushmen of the Kalahari locating a buried ostrich egg full of emergency water, stashed perhaps years ago in a landscape devoid of trees, rivers, roads, or other distinguishing marks. The desert shows us that the emptiest and most apparently desolate places are filled with life.

Wrote Laurie in one of my workshops, "This desert landscape terrifies me with its barrenness, but if I can be patient, if I can take the gift of time it offers me to really see it, I know that I will find a well within me from which to drink."

You are here to find your own trail through the desert. Perhaps, like Laurie, you feel frightened and lost. Perhaps you have forgotten who you are or where you are headed. You, too, may need to find the thread of your song again. Stripped of the usual assurances, you may enter the desert bearing the question "Am I enough just as I am?" The wind, the space, the dryness, answer.

We find our internal music by discovering who we are in our deepest beings, when everything else is taken away. We don't go to the desert to be more or make more, but to find the beauty and magnificence that are already within us.

Consider the spade-footed toad with his bright yellow eyes. During long hot spells he covers himself in desert sand to stay moist. Burrowed under the earth, he can survive for months in a state equivalent to hibernation. Yet the cue for the adult toad to emerge during summer thunderstorms is not moisture, but rather a low-frequency sound or vibration, probably caused by rainfall or thunder. The toad, I like to believe, hears his own songline calling to him, and he rises to the surface proclaiming, "Here I am. Here I am."

In the vast and arid desert it is miracle enough to simply be.

Emptiness Exploration

Carve out two hours or longer in your schedule to spend time alone and make a collage. You're about to create your own songline.

For this exploration, you will need a blank piece of paper or board (9" x 12" or larger), several magazines with different kinds of images, a small pile of paper cut into slender, half-inch strips, and a glue stick.

Begin by sitting quietly and turning your awareness to your own body. Listen to your breath, your heartbeat, and if you're outside, the way the wind and sun feel against your skin.

Each time you notice something about yourself—a thought, an emotional tug, or a physical sensation—write it down briefly on a slip of paper, without judgment.

When you feel complete, take a look at the phrases and intuitively arrange them in any order that feels right to you.

Your songline might go something like this:

Hunger in my belly,

Sadness inside . . .

Galaxies of thoughts swirl inside me

I feel solid like stone, warmed by the sun . . .

Next, cut out any images from the magazines that seem to reflect the emotional landscape of your words. You are ready to create your beautiful "songline" collage.

As you create your collage, take a moment to notice how lush, lovely, strange, and quirky you are. Notice the emotional tone of your images and phrases. What does the overall ground of your being feel like in this moment?

When your collage is complete, find a quiet place away from the world to sing your song.

Jot down any additional reflections you want to capture in your journal.

CHAPTER 6

Impermanence

We all begin as a bundle of bones lost somewhere in the desert.

–Clarissa Pinkola Estés

In the desert, more than in any other landscape, death is exposed. The cactus and the Joshua tree bear witness to the white bones all around them, bones that don't easily decompose in air absent of moisture. Drought and searing heat are other reminders that life is precious and will not last forever.

Caroline Brumleve, a participant in one of my workshops, put it this way: "You could so easily walk out into that dryness and into the arms of death. Or you could simply lie down and wait."

It was nearly 105 degrees, the sky so bright I felt I'd landed on the planet of ten suns. I was walking through the Badlands of South Dakota. I've heard it told of mountaineers that at altitude they can slowly drop off to sleep, and here I was in a haze of heat, almost doing the same. As if lying down wouldn't be such a bad idea after all. Returning to the car, I was shocked to find that my CamelBak, which had contained almost two liters of water when I started out on my six-mile hike, was empty.

To inhabit this parched Earth is always an act of faith. We may long to succumb to the seductions of the mirage: the illusion that we can escape our own end, live forever, never get sick or lose what or whom we love. But when we find the courage to confront the inevitability of loss, the desert offers amazing gifts of grace and growth.

The desert shows us that the nature of all things is impermanence. Here the landscape of sand dunes shifts with a sudden wind; great dust clouds bite into rock, sculpting it into strange and ceaselessly changing shapes. One flash flood can re-form the entire terrain in a moment. Life is not just a journey to the one big death, but a series of losses that continually change us, alter the very landscapes we inhabit.

We come to the desert to explore what death is, to walk among the bones.

Putting death at the center of our lives might seem morbid. But spend time in the desert and you will soon think otherwise. Here, wildflowers go from seed to seed in six short weeks, but they make such a showing in that time they are not to be pitied. The spade-footed toad spends his passion in two short days, his sheep-like *baaas* drowning out the silence before he disappears underground. But what a raucous celebration of life it is.

"To me they are as beautiful as anything I know," Georgia O'Keeffe said of the sun-bleached bones and skulls she found in the desert.[1] But equally amazing to her were the voluptuous flowers she painted. And isn't this the essential paradox of the desert? In acknowledging the reality of death, and our own transience, as perhaps no other creature can, we are awakened to the preciousness of life.

This was made to clear to me in May of 2009 when I said good-bye to Elizabeth, who had been my close friend and creative champion for more than three years. I went to see her with Annie and Lee, the other two members of our writing group. Her black hair now a thin shock of white, she lay in bed under a window, the radiance of the day illuminating her body.

I had brought my camera, and Elizabeth's sister took pictures of the four of us—Elizabeth, Annie, Lee, and me. When I loaded the photos onto my computer later that day, all I could see was Elizabeth's luminosity, her amazing beauty and grace transcending the ravages of cancer. It was if all the light of the world had gathered inside her.

I had rarely felt so sad as when I left her house knowing I would never see her again. Or so hungry for life.

We can expend so much energy in denying death: building our lives around security, trying to keep ourselves safe. Like tourists speeding through the desert with the AC cranked high, we imagine ourselves inured to the dangers around us.

But when we allow the desert to break through our denial, we may discover a surprising devil-may-care attitude arising. We may experience a new freedom. We may decide that in the face of life's brevity, like the spade-footed toad, we had better live all out.

Impermanence Exploration

Write a letter to yourself, written by the "you" at the end of your life to the "you" in the present moment. Imagine what your end-of-life self would have to say about how you're living your life now. Are you living full out? Are you living bravely and freely? Allow your end-of-life self to lovingly share what she or he sees and feels about how fully you're embracing your life. As you reflect back on what you've written, ask yourself what changes you will need to make in order to have lived your life "all out." Record your answers in your journal.

∽ Leaving the Deserts ∽

You are leaving the desert, at least for the moment. Now is the time to capture any realizations that came to you during your time here. What did you learn about yourself? Have your feelings about the desert and your own soul changed? What would you add to the desert soulscape that we haven't covered here?

Allow yourself to feel into your experience. What new behaviors or habits do you feel committed to adopting, or to giving up? If you were to live a full expression of your desert soul, what would that look like?

What most calls you to the desert? Is there any place that still feels frightening or off-putting? If so, why? Is there any place that you are drawn to exploring more deeply?

Don't edit. Simply allow yourself to reflect upon this vital relationship.

You'll come back to the desert many times in your life. Spending time reflecting on this journey now will allow you to track your growth over time.

PART 2
Forests

I will speak to you in forest language,
answer with the roots of dreams.

The clearest way into the Universe is through
a forest wilderness.

–John Muir

Forests comprise 30 percent of Earth's land surface. The rainforests of the Amazon, home to the richest ecosystem outside of the oceans, have been called the lungs of the planet. Forests take many shapes and forms: the soaring redwoods of California; the broad-leaved woodlands of Vermont that change so dramatically with the seasons; the brooding boreal forests of the Northern Hemisphere, home to wolves, tigers, and bears.

It was in the forest that our primate ancestry took root and human evolution began in earnest. Our hands knew bark and branch long before they picked up spear and spanner. In the forests our brains developed, with the manual dexterity and spatial acuity we attained clambering among tree limbs, and this later allowed us to put our imaginations to play in the material world. When we talk of the "mother tree," we recognize an essential truth: trees helped raise us.

Forests are deeply rooted in our imaginations and psyches—the sacred trees that formed the first ancient ritual sites; the Bodhi tree where the Buddha found enlightenment; the beautiful and threatened cedar forest in the story of Gilgamesh; the Tree of Life, the universal symbol that connects Heaven and Earth. Forests abound in myths and fairytales, in dark woods filled with witches, demons, and spells, in the wise crone we often meet there and Little Red Riding Hood, who must traverse the woods and use her wits to survive.

We carry forests within our spirits and memories—the tree that cradled us through the storms of childhood, our love for all things green and verdant, our yearning for mystery and magic and wisdom—in the shadow and the light of us.

For some, the forest is a comforting landscape. A client of mine, a grandmother, is learning to share her wisdom after being silenced for a long time by a punitive church. She keeps dreaming that she lives in the woods. "Trees enfold me. They give me a feeling of being cradled in the womb," she tells me. But for others a forest is a frightening place where we find ourselves off track, far from home. Trunks and branches crowd out the view. Roots cover the path. Amid canopy and cover we find we have lost our way. Writes Dante in the famous opening lines of the "Divine Comedy":

In the middle of the journey of our life,
I found myself in a dark wood;
for the straight way was lost.[1]

Any event that takes us off the straight and narrow path, the well-traveled track, can propel us into the forest. As one woman told me shortly after losing her job, "It is the corridors, the in-between places in life that frighten me." You may find yourself in the forest soulscape when one door closes behind you and another has yet to open. This not-knowing, the feeling that something lurks in the shadows, can be terrifying. In the forest much is sensed but not always seen.

But forests are also an invitation to breathe the "wild air, world-mothering air," as the poet Gerard Manley Hopkins describes it.[2] Forests help Earth to breathe, and they have the capacity to inspire us as well, a word that comes from the Latin *spiritus*—breath.

In the forest, our creativity rises like sap: we are explorers, never knowing what we will find. There is a richness and diversity of life in rainforests that mirrors the incredible depth and breadth of our own souls. With the future and past hidden from sight, we stand in a present moment pulsating with possibilities. We learn to live the questions rather than rush the answers.

"Not till we are lost . . .," writes Thoreau, "do we begin to understand ourselves."[3] Making our home in the forest, we embrace complexity and uncertainty. We learn to live from our wits and instinct. We leave the well-marked roads, the signposts, the straight path, entering instead the place of natural geometry, spiraling trails, rippling roots, tangled branches. We are less certain. But we are more alive. We awaken to something deeper.

Imagine you are standing at the edge of a vast forest. This side of it, you are caught in the whirl of modern life with its smart phones, freeway traffic, droning airplanes, and ceaseless demands to make money, pay bills, get ahead. But in front of you lies uncharted terrain—wild, unfettered, and vast beyond imagining. It is the place of your forest soul. And it is waiting to be explored.

CHAPTER 7

Mystery

You enter the forest at the darkest point,
where there is no path.

–Joseph Campbell

I asked a soft-spoken man in his late twenties who had just spent the summer introducing inner-city kids to the Oregon forests, "Did they love being outdoors?"

"No," he replied. "They were terrified."

He said that these children, many of whom live in neighborhoods that resemble war zones, saw the forest as infinitely more threatening than bullet-ridden streets. "One kid," he said, "shrieked with horror when a branch brushed against him. He went berserk."

It was after ten o'clock at night, and I was returning to my cabin nestled amid the redwood trees at a retreat center in the hills above Santa Cruz. I had been teaching a class on writing called "The Root Voice," and I was ready for sleep. But the air was warm, the stars brilliant, and, with everyone in bed, the night tranquil. I turned away from my cabin and walked deeper into the woods.

Above me, the wind in the treetops filled the sky with the ocean's roar. Beneath my feet, the Earth spun black as the heavens, so that the trees seemed to grow out of the sky and the ground simultaneously. Blackness wrapped around me and the damp earth, with its mix of sharp pine and dank scent. I heard the snap of branches, the crackle of dry pine needles; imagined eyes lighting up the forest like starlight. An owl screeched, beak and claw tearing into the night. Everything soft in me trembled.

I could have headed back to the safety of my cabin there and then, but like a child enthralled by a scary fairytale I was pulled toward the enchanted world of the dark forest. I was five years old again, listening to my father weave yarns of witches, dark woods, and decaying castles. I sought out the scary places back then in Grimm's fairy tales, read late at night by flashlight, inviting ghosts, goblins, and giants to follow me into my dreams. And I sought the scary places again that night as the moonless forest enfolded me.

The forest is the darkest of the landscapes. Trees press in. Dense foliage blocks the compass sun from view. No longer able to depend on our sense of sight, our other senses become more acute. Hackles raised, instincts awakened, we move out of the clear-cut life into uncharted places. If we enter without a map, or a road, we make a path through the forest that is entirely our own.

When I was a little girl I often played in Holland Park in London. Not the wild woods, exactly, but with enough leafy chestnut trees and sinister-seeming corners to infuse me with excitement. Darkness is dangerous. But it also holds wonder and magic. It brings us closer to the ultimate mystery of things. Immersed in darkness, our imaginative powers grow. We conjure the light with clay, claw, and pen.

If you have ever dared to brave the depths of your creativity, you know the power of darkness—know the world is a mystical and mercurial place. In the forest you glimpse a flash of feathers in the boughs, a paw print in the dirt, and you are graced. But you are also stalked. Something out there is seeking you too. It will only reveal itself if the moment is right.

Entering the woods, you are as much the hunted as the hunter. Lines of poetry pursue you; ideas and images track you. Beneath the shadowy trunks of trees, visions unfurl. A fallen log becomes a bear; a snake's camouflage disappears her back into the forest; a hummingbird is there . . . is gone.

Did you see it? Was it real?

The wisdom you seek here can be experienced but never possessed. Wild, ancient, primal, it moves through the shadows. The presence of such mystery and immensity is overwhelming. You may have to fight the urge to break the tension by running away. But if you remain, at least for a while, things will happen. In this uncertain world, creativity flourishes.

We may seek straight paths and the straightforward approach, but it is a Universe both circular and shrouded that shapes us. Physicists tell us that dark matter and dark energy comprise 95 percent of the Universe. With all our technologies, all our instruments, we have observed less than 5 percent of the cosmos. What scientists have measured, we sense with our souls. Entering the forest, we know we are bound by darkness, born into mystery.

The light of modern consciousness burns brightly, but the Earth was never meant to be bare of trees, nor our souls fully exposed to the light of reason. We are meant to include some element of uncharted terrain in our makeup. A clear-cut area becomes drier and less fertile with time, just as we, too, are diminished by a modern mind-set that wants to elevate rational thought and industry at the expense of vision and spirit.

Those inner-city kids understood what it was to face the fears of the daytime, the ugly underbelly of urban life. But the branch that touches like a cold hand, the overgrown path, the spirit of the land—that is another matter. We have lost our ability to imagine beyond the prescribed maps we have been handed. We have forgotten the power of our own wildness.

Mystery is wild. All forests hold an element of danger. What you run into can be menacing, even deadly. A wild creature can kill you. You can set out and become dangerously lost. But if you take the mystery out of life, you squeeze out your capacity to marvel. Avoiding risk, you bypass magic.

As I walked that night in the redwood forest on the hills above Santa Cruz, I knew mountain lions roamed close by. The staff at the retreat center had told me it was dangerous to walk alone after twilight.

I peered into the gloaming forest, perceived shadows prowling in the underbrush, felt the hair on my neck rising. So when something moved in the trees, I was certain what it was. I screamed.

What emerged that night in the forest wasn't the fierce and predatory creature of my imagination, but rather a tiny white moth, luminous, coming toward me on wings both delicate and strong.

Imagination flitters through us like this—always surprising, always wondrous. And we search for it in the darkness.

Mystery Exploration

Make friends with mystery. Explore a trail by moonlight, or sit in your back garden or inside your home at night with all the lights turned off.

Give your eyes time to adjust to the darkness. Feel your senses, other than eyesight, begin to take over. Can you sense prickles on your skin? Or the way sounds stand out? How is your awareness shifting and expanding?

Spend as much time in the darkness as you are comfortable with, and then just a little bit longer.

Then, with the aid of a flashlight or candlelight, pick up your journal and begin a fifteen-minute freewrite with these words:

"This is what I sense is trying to find me right now . . ."

Let your thoughts flow through your pen onto the page, however crazy or disjointed they might feel.

Note: Depending on how safe your neighborhood is, please adapt this exploration to ensure that no harm comes to you. A night hike can be a safe and bonding experience when friends and family join in. Just remember to enroll everyone in the process, and walk in silence.

CHAPTER 8

Wisdom

Today I have grown taller from walking with the trees.

–Karle Wilson Baker

The tree is god, she told her daughter. You must not cut him down. Every day the young girl walked by the god tree on her way to get water. The daughter came to revere the tree, learned how he helped keep the stream clean—the stream that held pearls of tadpole eggs and the life-giving water she brought home. Then the white people came and took down all the trees and put up a church instead. The god tree was gone. And so the stream dried up and the frogs died, and the land became barren.

The little girl in that story was Wangari Maathai, Nobel Peace Prize winner and founder of the Greenbelt Movement in Kenya. Today, her organization has helped plant over 40 million trees in Kenya and other countries. Like the ancient god tree she revered as a child, she became a true elder—one who lived to serve the community.

Wangaari Maathai died of ovarian cancer in 2011, but her legacy lives on. This is what elders do: they serve the needs of the young and the vulnerable. Old trees do this and elder humans do this.

And both are being cut down.

The old stumps of dead trees always capture my attention. I imagine that I am tiny, just three inches tall, and am looking up at them. The

31

wood is a cliff wall covered in moss and feathery leaves, crumbling and cracking. I have entered an enchanted world. The hollow trunks are cavernous, and I watch in awe as fungi, beetles, bats, and birds find refuge in these realms. Some of these snags were once soaring redwood trees, as high as 360 feet tall: towering kings of the coastal forest. Now they live close to the ground.

There is something absolutely magnificent about walking in a full-growth forest, when light shines through the needles and leaves in great shimmering columns; the way our heads tilt up from time to time, almost involuntarily, pulled by the sway of the treetops like masts at sea. But it is the low-lying trees, the broken and dissolving, that often convey a deeper sense of what it means to grow into a true elder—to open up, to become emptied of ego.

Does the hollowing out happen invisibly and in private? And how do we age with an open heart when we are so often encouraged to stay perpetually youthful? In a culture that values surfaces, how do we pay attention to what is unfolding within our depths?

I sit by an elder tree on the hill above my house. His body is slowly disintegrating, becoming fertile ground for new plants and trees. It is as if the tree is willing himself to be used up for the good of the Earth. I like to imagine that my increasingly arthritic hips and aging flesh are not an end unto themselves but a portal into a more generous and wiser time in my life.

After all, youth is the time for ego—a time to build up a sense of self. But true elderhood is a different matter entirely. Instead of worrying so much about staying young, perhaps we need to learn how to grow old. There is nothing more beautiful than an ancient tree with low branches that open like arms, embracing us. We need arms like that to hold us in these turbulent times.

For me, in the human world, that safe shelter was my grandfather. I can still recall my delight at his magic tricks, but it was his willingness to take me seriously that mattered most. One Christmas, when I was around eight years old and my brother, David, eleven, he opened a bottle of Crimean port and poured a thimbleful for both of us. Some of the adults gathered around the holiday table felt this exceptional port ought not to be wasted on us, but my grandfather wanted us to experience something both rare and delicious.

For an elder to take a child seriously is an extraordinary and wonderful thing. It helps us feel seen and acknowledged in a way we can't get from our peers, or even our parents. There is a long and life-giving umbilical cord that runs from the very old to the very young, and it is a vital part of any healthy family.

In old-growth forests, grandmother trees, whose roots spread across large sweeps of the forest floor, provide nutrients to younger, growing trees through a complex underground network. Ancient Douglas firs drop lobaria—a kind of lichen—onto the ground, turning nitrates into nitrogen that nurtures the young saplings. Failing to protect ancient groves, viewing elder trees as offering nothing special beyond their value as timber, we compromise the entire forest community.

Time and again, nature shows us that ancient wisdom has intrinsic worth above and beyond the new.

Jerry Mander, in his book *In The Absence of the Sacred,* writes that Canadian wildlife managers demanded the Inuit of Arctic Canada reduce their hunting by only killing full-grown male caribou, and only a few from each herd. The Inuit argued against this method. They said that it ignored the importance of the older animals to the survival of the caribou. Tragically, they were proved right: the caribou herd numbers dropped dramatically once the law was put into effect. It turned out the older animals possessed not only essential experience but also an ability to affect the emotional well-being of the herd. In their presence the pregnant females and the nervous young—the most vulnerable members of the herd—were calmer and more at ease.[1]

Youthful intelligence builds drones and clones, genetically modifies crops, develops new ways of gathering information, and performs experiments on Mars. It is full of ingenuity and innovation. Elder wisdom offers a different perspective. It isn't seduced by the new and powerful. Rather, it is dedicated to timeless principles that serve the welfare of the entire Earth community, especially the most at risk.

My client Katie is a perfect example. She came to me because she longs, in her mid-eighties, to finally access the power of her inner wild. She tells me that she wants to become what Clarissa Pinkola Estés deems a "Dangerous Old Woman."

"What does that mean to you?" I ask.

She turns her bright blues eyes on me. "It means to me the same thing it means to Clarissa, being the 'protector of even the tiniest spark of life.'"

Katie, like Wangari Maathai, like the aging caribou, like my grandfather, like the grandmother tree, wants to share her knowledge in a loving and encompassing way—not for her own advancement but in service of all beings. We need to embrace our elder wisdom, to become a culture of carers, to root ourselves in the depth of compassion.

I am reminded of Katie and all true elders whenever I look at a photo taken of me in the forests of the Quetrihué Peninsula in Argentina. Surrounded by towering arrayán trees, many more than three hundred years old, my face is peaceful, my eyes raised in reverence. I remember the dripping rain, the soft glow of the cinnamon-colored bark, the long twisting trunks, and a feeling that at any time I could be assumed into the towering tree branches as if lifted into heaven. Among these ancient and almost extinct beings, I am encircled by wisdom.

There is no other word for it.

Wisdom Exploration

Do you remember a grandmother or grandfather tree from your childhood? Was there a particular tree that stands out in your memory—in whose arms you felt safe and sheltered?

If you can't recall a grandparent tree from your youth, simply search out a tree in a local park or neighborhood that holds elder energy. Or look for an image of an elder tree in a magazine.

When you're ready, write a character sketch of your chosen tree in all her many details: texture, smell, distinguishing marks, height, shape, and demeanor. Describe the tree with rich attention to how she appears to you and the way that you felt (or feel) in her presence.

What is it that draws you to this particular tree? What energy emanates from her? When you've completed writing your character sketch, take a moment to answer this question:

"In what ways does this tree teach me about how I want to grow into my elderhood?"

Write your response in your journal.

CHAPTER 9

Uniqueness

For everything that lives is holy.

–William Blake

In the rainforest of the Amazon, the mighty Brazil tree owes his life to the small agouti rat, whose teeth are the only things sharp enough to crack the hard nutshells, enabling the tree to reproduce. Without this tiny creature, the tallest tree in this tall forest, the one that towers over all the others, couldn't survive.

The forest teaches us that by being fully ourselves, however seemingly small and insignificant, we enable the web of life to thrive.

You walk into the forest and everything hushes.

Every morning, when I head up the hill into the mix of coast live oaks, bay laurels, and madrones above my house, it is as if I'm a stern parent interrupting a teenager's party. My presence causes the forest to go quiet. Deer spring away, birds halt their scuffling in the undergrowth, a coyote lopes out of range. A whipsnake, in a final act of defiance, curls the tip of its pointed tail at me, forming a perfect pink coral shell, and then vanishes into the grasses.

I feel immeasurably blessed by this daily reminder of how much life exists in forests. Among the most diverse regions on Earth, forests remind us that healthy ecosystems contain a vast multiplicity of life-forms. Rainforests, crucibles of diversity, contain more than half of all species on Earth.

Knowing who we are and what we alone have to offer is essential to living our lives fully and well. But in a world that seeks our conformity more than it desires our gifts, we often must struggle to be true to ourselves. Unlike the tiny agouti with its peculiarly sharp teeth, we often neglect to develop our innate and unique talents, and the larger world suffers from that self-neglect. Rather, we shape ourselves to fit the world as we see it to be, or as we are told it is, hoping to ensure our welcome and sense of purpose that way.

But nature wants us to mix it up. In old-growth climax forests that have been allowed to evolve without interference, diversity thrives. There's a snake in the jungles of Southeast Asia that can fly three hundred feet through the air. Now, we all know snakes can't fly. But it seems no one told the paradise tree snake, so it went about perfecting the art, launching its long green body like a streamer from a high tree branch, tail raised, body flattened out to ride the air currents.

The redwoods that tower near my home proclaim through their fractal beauty, that they are both unique and part of a whole pattern of existence, much as we humans are. Being open to our true nature—what we emerged from Earth for—is ultimately an act of faith.

But nature is purposeful. The Earth needs your gifts.

This became very clear in a dream that came to me as I slept on the forest floor on the far northern island of Cortes in British Columbia, soothed to sleep by the tiny crackle of insects, the rustle of leaves, and the musty fragrance of wet earth.

I am inside a large white tent filled with young boys dressed in wool coats, cloth caps, and stout boots. One by one, they move to the center of the tent to dance upon mandalas. Each taps out an aboriginal-style painting with his boots, creating an intricate and unique pattern within the sacred circle.

Another boy begins to dance. I look at my watch and say, "We don't have time for this." That's when I see the First Nation elders.

They encircle the tent, long white hair falling almost to the floor, heads thrown back in pure joy at the boys' dancing.

A yellow dog appears with a wide red stripe down his face. His fierce eyes lock on mine. In that moment I know: there is nothing more important than being able to dance our unique dance.

Later, I read of Jung's work on the mandala, that he noticed its appearance in all cultures across the globe. And that in each instance, the mandala represents the connection between the whole and the part: the unity of life and the myriad ways in which it is expressed. In a similar vein, Eve Ensler asks us to consider what might happen if we were to ". . . find freedom, aliveness, and power not from what contains, locates, or protects us, but from what dissolves, reveals, and expands us."[1] Could it be that in honoring our particular nature, in celebrating and owning fundamentally who we are, we claim our place in the world?

The soul's evolution thrives on uniqueness, and the evolution of the Earth depends on diversity. We are not all created to live identical lives. When we follow the inclination of our own souls, we become like the small trap-jaw ant in the jungle whose bite is more powerful, literally, than that of a shark. No one told this ant that being small meant being impotent. Nor do we know what we are capable of until we let go of the expectations of others.

In 1955 in Alabama, when a woman refused to sit at the back of a bus because her particular soul refused such indignity, she could never have known that hers would become one of the most powerful acts of civil disobedience in modern history. The word "unique" comes from the Latin for "one." But it also carries another meaning—something rare or remarkable, something absolutely extraordinary.

The other day I saw a tiny creature while walking with a friend in the woods. Poking his head out of a pile of leaves was a frog, half the size of my thumb. We knelt to get a closer look, our heads bowed as if in prayer.

We might never see this amazing being again.

Uniqueness Exploration

No two trees are the same. See how each bends, leafs, and grows according to her own nature. As you wander your neighborhood, or head for a local wooded area or park, simply observe how each tree you come across is distinct and different. When you feel yourself pulled toward a certain tree, sketch the shape and form of the tree in your journal. Don't worry if you're not a very good artist; sketching the tree will help you observe her more keenly. After you've sketched the tree, take a moment to reflect:

How is this tree unique?

What drew me to this tree rather than the others?

What shape does my soul take when I celebrate and express my uniqueness?

CHAPTER 10

Shadow

What we are doing to the forests of the world is but a mirror reflection of what we are doing to ourselves and to one another.

–Mahatma Gandhi

Is this how trees feel when they've been cut down?

I had been researching deforestation for this book when I became sick. One night, my temperature soared to 104 degrees and I passed out in my bathroom. When I returned to consciousness, I found myself face down, my nose smashed against the track of the shower door. I felt the stickiness of blood all around me.

As I lay there, helpless and in pain, a thought popped into my fevered brain: "I am like a tree that has been cut down." I curled up on the cool floor, not yet ready or able to rise. I wept for myself, and all the trees in the fallen forests.

For days after my fainting spell, I felt shaky. My nose in the mirror, like a coat hook, was clearly broken, yet I couldn't bring myself to see a doctor. Instead, now that my fever had passed, I tried to push through with my writing and workshop schedule. But I couldn't find the rhythm. I felt stuck. And the more stuck I felt, the harder I pushed.

One sunny day, frustrated by my lack of progress, I hiked up the hill on a trail I regularly take, packing along my journal. At the top of the hill, down a side trail, I felt drawn to sit in the arms of a great black oak, gnarled and lichen-covered. I sat astride a wide branch, my back pressed against the grainy trunk.

Bees droned by. The wind streamed soft and warm, and the occasional scuffle of tiny birds in the leaves was hypnotic. I smelled the bark, fragrant and ripe in the sunshine; watched tiny ants scurrying back and forth along the branches.

My breath eased and my body relaxed. I took out my journal and began a dialogue with the tree, starting, as I frequently do, with a simple request:

Mary: *Mother tree, will you talk with me?*

Tree: *Yes, my child.*

Mary: *I'm sorry I haven't been more present for you recently. I seem to be consumed by my own struggles.*

Tree: *Yes, I miss the joy that usually emanates from you.*

Mary: *I'm devastated by what humans are doing to your brothers and sisters. I felt it in my own soul when I collapsed the other week.*

Tree: *It is painful, isn't it? To be upright and rooted one moment, crashing helplessly to the ground the next. Thank you for feeling this with me.*

Mary: *But why can't I move past this feeling? Why so much pain around all this?*

Tree: *Perhaps there's more for you to learn.*

Mary: *Like what?*

In the pause that followed, I felt the air vibrate, almost hum.

Tree: *You sometimes treat yourself—and others—the same way as those who cut down the forest treat the trees. You look for shortcuts and expediencies. You want answers* now. *That's a kind of clear-cutting. And it is a brutal way to live.*

My hand halted above my journal. What was the tree communicating to me? But I knew. I'd been so stressed, just trying to get the next thing done, I was undermining the dark, leafy knowing inside of me—the part of me connected to the natural rhythms and mysteries of Earth. Intent on progress, I couldn't make peace with the present moment, however unfinished or unformed it might be. I had no faith, except in my own ability to get things done. I was clear-cutting my way through life.

As I leaned into the tree, a deep sadness pervaded me for all of us who are so caught up in the stresses of modern life that we fail to appreciate the simple beauty of the present, seemingly imperfect moment. I could see control and domination, not just as something that affected the world of forests but as the energy that ran my own life. When I'm hell-bent on trying to ensure a certain outcome or accomplish some task, I am never happy, never satisfied, always in pursuit.

Out of the shadow and into the light came a knowing that this forceful energy was at the root of so much destruction and hurt in the world, and in my own life. Indeed, I had used it against myself, pushing myself to the limits as I looked for shortcuts, unwilling to trust to the forest's winding path.

I sat against the tree for a long time, simply resting in her arms and thanking her for her blessing and her wisdom. In me, a desire took root: to heal my own dominator energy so my work could spring naturally, from deep inside. I longed for this with all my heart: for the forests to thrive and the untamed, tangled terrain of my soul—of all our souls—to flourish as well.

I looked around at the dappled light and mix of thick groves of trees and small clearings, becoming lost in the shimmering dance of brilliance and shadow. All around me the sky-tipped branches and hidden roots reminded me of the darkness and the light. They are within us too.

A week later, I went to see the doctor. He had to break my nose again and reset it. It still carries a little bump, so that now my own face is slightly gnarled, like tree bark. Every time I look in the mirror, I'm reminded to surrender my will to a deeper, more natural energy. A fair exchange, I believe, for a less than perfect nose.

Shadow Exploration

Approach a tree respectfully and ask to settle in beside her for a while. Note your mood. Are you calm and at ease? Are you carrying any anxiety with you? Are you happy or angry?

Begin your dialogue with the tree by asking, *"What's important for me to know about the way I'm feeling right now?"*

Allow the conversation to flow between you, writing both your questions and the tree's responses in your journal. Don't worry if you feel a little strange at first. If the conversation slows, simply prompt the tree with such questions as "Is there more for me to see and understand? What else can you share with me?"

When you have thanked the tree for her wisdom, notice: have your feelings become clearer, or have they lifted? If so, how?

You will want to take some time to summarize what you have learned from the tree. What wisdom have you gleaned from the conversation? Whatever you discover, know that we are all creatures of light and shadow. This isn't about right and wrong. It is about owning the fullness of who we are.

Record your reflection in your journal.

CHAPTER 11

Rootedness

Be like a tree. Stay rooted in the dream
that breathed you here.

–Lauren de Boer

It is late summer, and I lean against a giant sequoia in Muir Grove in Sequoia National Park. Some of the trees in this particular grove have been here for more than two thousand years; some may remain for another thousand or more. "Wherever a seed lands, its fate is sealed," writes David Suzuki in *Tree: A Life Story.*[1] Whatever approaches the tree, from predators to insects to deadly diseases or the cut of the chainsaw, has to be accepted. Escape is not an option.

Native Americans call the trees Standing People. Trees share with humans the "vertical" life, only they remain in place from birth to death. Except perhaps for a very strange group of trees somewhere on a Pacific island that are reported to lift up their roots and inch along the earth year by year. But they are the exception. Trees, in the main, hold their ground.

Being stationary requires ingenuity. Some trees contort themselves into incredible pretzel shapes in order to push through the crowded canopy around them and receive their share of sunlight. Their roots, likewise, may adapt by exhibiting a marvelous roaming spirit. They dig deep in the earth, move laterally, bond with mycorrhizal fungi that enable them to seek moisture and sustenance from farther afield, all while maintaining their position.

44

Trees have learned to live large, despite constraints. They have all kinds of rich relationships, too, with the birds and insects and other beings that seek out their branches and nest in their hollowed trunks. "I like trees because they seem more resigned to the way they have to live than other things do," writes Willa Cather.[2]

In a world of restless motion, trees restore us to stillness and calm. Entering a forest is like entering a cathedral. And vice versa. Gothic cathedrals, with their lofty, ribbed vaults, recall the leafy roofs and towering trunks of the sacred groves where humans first worshipped. In both places, we stand in awe.

Muir Grove, host to the giant sequoia tree I rest against, is one of the most spectacular stands of sequoias I have witnessed. I have hiked here with a group I am leading on an "Inner Wild" retreat. We entered by way of a lush forest path, past rocky outcrops and a profusion of carriage-size ferns, serenaded by the whispering song of the hermit thrush. Then, suddenly, the whole group stilled and quieted. Nothing can prepare you for the sight of these giants rising rich, red, and monumental from the forest floor. They stop you; root you.

Imagine trunks wide as roads that take a small choir of people to circle them. Or bark the color of caramel apples. Imagine the height of a thirty-story building and branches that only emerge above 160 feet. Imagine trees thirty-two times the body weight of a blue whale and three times as long. And still, describing the dimensions of a sequoia is like saying Gandhi was five feet five, skinny, and wore glasses. The energy emitted from these beings cannot be conveyed by mere measurements. Among the oldest organisms on Earth, the sequoias' lineage stretches back 144 million years, to when dinosaurs roamed the land. These ancient sentinels command your presence.

As the group disperses to find special places to journal, I think about how I always want to change my life not from within, but from without. It is easier to start something new than work on completing what I've begun. I've held scores of jobs and live six thousand miles from where I was born and have been married three times. I have lived in so many homes I can barely recall them all. I have walked almost every trail in Marin County where I live, and many others, from the Himalayas to the Andes, because I like different views and surprises. Restlessness is part of my nature.

But sometimes all that movement is more about leaving things behind than actually arriving somewhere new. In 12-step recovery we call it "doing a geographic." You move because you don't have the guts to confront what's right in front of you, which is mostly the mess of your own creation. How many of us run from some aspect of life?

Yet in this moment, with the towering sequoia at my back, restlessness seems almost childish. Surrounded by these gentle forest giants, I feel what those who've made lifelong friends with meditation most likely feel: a sense of profound calm.

And I wonder what would happen if we learned to be this still. Would we learn to adapt to the reality of our situation? What new roots might we send down? What webs of connection would we discover? How truly majestic could our spirits grow to be if we simply stood our ground, for ourselves, each other, and the Earth?

Drifting ever onward has for so long seemed the easier option. But that time has come and gone. We are one people, on one tiny orb, in a vast Universe. What happens to one happens to us all. We cannot run away from the chaos and destruction we're creating. There is no "away" anymore.

I realize it is time to stop all this frantic motion, both personal and global. The search for the next frontier, this belief that one more invention, one more technology, or one more relationship is all we need to solve our problems, keeps us from the consequences of our behaviors.

Instead, we would do better to do as the trees do:

Learn to stand still.

Rootedness Exploration

Find a quiet spot in nature, preferably in the presence of trees, where you can take off your shoes and plant your feet soundly on the ground, about hip width apart. Imagine roots extending from the soles of your feet deep into the earth, burrowing through into the mulch and damp soil.

If you're comfortable, raise your arms like tree branches and gently move them back and forth, as if swaying in a breeze. Feel the sunlight warming your limbs; sense the moisture and minerals rising up in you from the ground. Allow yourself to feel fed from above and nurtured from below. Sense how strong your roots are.

Feel the Earth pulling you into alignment.

When you're ready, take out your journal and complete this prompt: "When I am rooted, I feel . . ."

Freewrite your response for five minutes, allowing whatever thoughts you have to flow without interruption onto the page.

Then ask, "What would be different if I met every challenge by becoming more rooted in myself and my place in the world?"

Write down your response.

CHAPTER 12

Emergence

I love the dark hours of my being.
My mind deepens into them.

–Rainer Maria Rilke

We burrow into the forest, hiding from the broad light of day, our poetic, wild mind waiting and biding its time. Sometimes our ideas need to remain underground for many years before they can become visible, take shape, and blossom into the light of the rational world. The word "emergence" comes from the Latin *emergere*, "bring to light."

Everything begins in darkness.

The soul is shy. It trembles in harsh light. Have you ever exposed an idea or dream prematurely? The slightest stirring of rejection or ridicule can kill it dead. Before being shared, your inner imaginings first need to be nurtured and grow strong within you. The forest soulscape—dark, protected, lush—is the perfect incubator.

The still of the morning, between the world of the unconscious and the conscious, is my forest hour. Half of me is still wrapped in reverie, and outside the light is soft and blurred, no hard edges. It is the time of the perfect soul light. Here is the in-between world, a liminal space where we stand between darkness and dawn, still hidden from the harsh glare of day.

A woman in one of my workshops said the first place she felt safe enough to write in her diary was in the forest that encircled her school. Hidden by trees, she was free to explore her hopes and dreams. Listening to her story, I knew exactly what she meant. My first journal was a bright pink diary with a gold lock on it; I kept the tiny gold key hidden in a drawer. My thoughts were tucked away from prying eyes— secured between those bright pink covers. We need a safe place to tend to the intimate urgings of our souls.

I sit in a forest, holding an acorn. The plum-colored outer shell is already breaking apart to reveal the next, thicker, flesh-colored layer. Soon, if conditions are right, this acorn will split open and out of it will emerge a leafless tendril, as spare and translucent as a new stem of asparagus. Thrusting through layers of old leaves and forest debris, this tiny oak tree will soon be recognizable for what it is.

As surely as the acorn contains the oak tree, so your dreams are held inside the womb of your soul. The poet T. S. Eliot claims that he wasn't so much aided by inspiration as by "the breaking down of strong habitual barriers—which tend to reform very quickly."[1] In order to break through the protective layers of ego and habit, your authentic being will have to grow strong. You are shedding skin, pushing through resistance, making way for something truer to emerge.

Writes the poet Rilke, "You must give birth to your images."[2] But images have form, and before there is form there is formlessness: an idea, a glimpse of something, an inclination. This is the time in the creative process when you can feel a flutter, delicate as moth wings, deep in your belly. It has no name, no shape, but still it stirs.

You may be the tentative kind who only gradually reveals more of your essential nature when you feel the conditions are safe to do so. You may be like the ferns after the 1995 Mount Vision fire at Point Reyes National Seashore that unfurled their brilliant green shoots out of the earth while the ground still smoldered. You may even rely on some cataclysmic event to crack you open, just as bishop pines require fire for their seeds to fly open, like tiny stars in the night.

There are many ways to be born, but life always emerges out of darkness.

We need dark and hidden realms where ideas can quietly take root, away from a timetable not of our soul's making. Away from the need so many feel in this reality-TV, social-media, YouTube world to be constantly on public display.

Awaiting the right time, the right conditions, demands that we be patient and remain alert. We need to work on the ground of our being, ready ourselves, soak in nourishment. Staying close to the earth, our ideas carry the assurance and strength of humility—an understanding of the sacred soil of our own essence.

Karen's story speaks to this directly. A woman in her fifties with the soul of a poet and mystic—two qualities our present world tends to undervalue—Karen is happiest living as an intuitive, a dream weaver, a healer. Only, for much of her life she's believed that if she revealed her true nature, she would be ridiculed.

When Karen was laid off from a job that offered her financial security, she was no longer able to afford the mortgage on her Berkeley house. Having spent months nurturing her inner creativity in our sessions together, when the time came, Karen didn't hesitate. She sold her house, moved to the Southwest, downsized dramatically, and now spends her time writing poetry and practicing as a healer.

The first half of Karen's life, as is true for so many, was spent growing her world on the outside in order to conform—house, job, respectability. Now she was ready to grow her life from the inside out. And with that choice, her true nature was finally revealed.

And so, you trust.

You listen.

You wait.

If the dream is strong, when the conditions are right, it will emerge out of the darkness to take its place in the world.

And so will you.

Emergence Exploration

What follows is a seven-step process to grow an oak tree from an acorn. Participating in this "emergence" will awaken you more deeply to what it takes to birth something new. You can also choose to plant any other kind of bulb or seed and monitor its growth. Or even watch the process happening naturally, all about you in the natural world.

My husband successfully planted an avocado pit. If you live in the pine forests, like a friend in Colorado does, you can always go to the nursery to find out about trees and plants better suited to your local terrain and weather.

Whatever you choose to plant and nurture, note the changes in your journal:

How does this process reflect your own creative process?

How is it different?

What are you learning about how your ideas go from seed to fruition, from darkness to daylight.

How to grow an oak tree:

1. Collect acorns in early fall. Ideally, the acorns should be brown or nearly black.

2. Place the acorns in a bucket of water for a couple minutes, discarding any that float.

3. Place the remaining acorns in a large zipper bag with damp sawdust; put them in your refrigerator for a month or longer, as needed to germinate the new oak.

4. Once the root has cracked through the acorn, it's ready to be planted.

5. Place each acorn in a two-inch diameter pot filled with soil, and deep enough so the taproot can grow. Place the acorn about two to four inches (five to ten centimeters) below the surface with the root facing down. Water regularly.

6. After each oak has grown about four inches (ten centimeters), which should take less than six months, they can be planted into the ground.

7. To transplant the oak seedlings into the ground from a pot, clear a three-foot circle of all vegetation.

Choosing where to transplant your tree in the ground is an action, and often a commitment, of lifelong significance. You will want to choose a spot for your oak tree (or other tree or plant) very carefully. Talk to someone in the know, so your tree (or plant) will have the optimal soil and space needed to grow.

∾ Leaving the Forests ∾

The forest, dark and full of mystery, lies behind you. As you prepare to venture forth, take a moment to consider your time spent wandering these leafy paths.

The forest represents a place of creative tension—we can become lost, find ourselves wandering in the darkness or waiting for something that is seeded to emerge.

What did you learn about your ability to hold this tension?

What did you learn about your ability to be rooted, to be wise?

Allow yourself to linger in the forest for a moment longer, noticing whether you're compelled to explore certain aspects more deeply. Or perhaps other forest paths beckoned that we didn't get to explore here. Maybe you're called to make your own path where none have gone before.

How will you continue to nurture the forest aspects of your soul?

PART 3
Oceans & Rivers

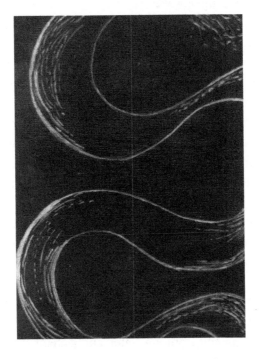

*I will speak to you in water language,
answer with the flow of river.*

Let yourself be silently drawn
by the stronger pull of what you really love.

–Jelal al-Din Rumi

Seventy percent of the planet is water. Seventy percent of your body is water. We evolved from an ancient sea of amniotic fluid. The eight thousand miles of arteries and veins that flow through our bodies are like the rivers and streams that circulate the Earth. Our heartbeats replicate the pounding of waves.

All of life arose from the primordial oceans. It was here that simple bacteria formed what later became tree, flower, bird. It was here that our ancestors sported fins as we now sport fingers. It was here, out of the swirling tides, that the first vertebrate made its way onto solid ground some 360 million years ago.

And it was from our mothers' salty wombs that we emerged into the world—each birth a small-scale reenactment of our evolutionary tale.

Water streams through our memories: our first swim, the lake we summered beside as children, the waves that buoyed us up and sucked us under. It is the carrier of tales—Odysseus setting sail for home; Noah building his ark for the flood; Captain Ahab chasing the great white whale; Huck Finn's escape to freedom on the Mississippi. Water conjures up images of sirens and Poseidon, healing pools and baptismal fonts.

Throughout history, humanity has congregated around big rivers like the Mississippi, Nile, and Thames. Sources of fish and fowl, fresh water for irrigation and drinking water, and a channel for commerce, rivers flow through the fabric of our lives. Equally called to the oceans, we also settle along the coastal edges of continents beside the great harbors and shipping lanes.

Water brings us alive both literally and figuratively. It pulses through the rills and channels of our bodies, arises from lust as saliva on our tongues, forms salty seas for swimming sperm. We experience water in steam, cloud, ice, rain, snow, flow. We experience it in the shape-shifting quality of existence, the ebb and flow of our enthusiasms, in the way we can shift from anger to love in an instant.

Losing our connection with our natural gifts and desires is like the ocean losing her connection with the moon, or the rivers their way to the sea. Something vital is lost. Listening to the innate urges of our deepest loves, we open to an inner flow. Often we experience it as a homecoming; to allow ourselves to venture into the waters, to *be long-ing,* leads us to the experience of *belonging* itself.

This soulscape is an invitation to explore what it is that pulls us and influences the flow of our lives. It is an invitation to move from the shallow waters of superficial thinking and doing into the depths of what is possible: for us, our communities, our fellow creatures, and for the Earth herself. But in order to do this, we must learn to navigate the many forms that longing can take—some destructive, some life-giving.

Navigating the oceans and rivers with skill, we become like the salmon; we know how to find our way to our sacred source; we know what feeds the tributaries of our inner being. We experience this soulscape as being in love—with life, work, spirit, another person. We are in the creative flow, full of juice and joy.

At times, however, this soulscape can be overwhelming. Perhaps we are vulnerable to excesses or addiction and easily swept away by desires that do not serve our souls. There are times we may find ourselves drowning in emotions. Banks cradle rivers; so, too, our energies benefit from being channeled to some particular purpose or commitment.

For many, letting go—being led by what we truly love—is the ultimate challenge. We've been taught to sublimate passion for duty, to do what is expedient or what others deem correct. As a result our natural desires can become culverted; they move underground.

A woman in her forties named Susan attended a Wild Soul workshop. I watched her light up with an idea for a moment, a huge smile aglow on her face; then, just as swiftly, she told me why it would never work, and the joy vanished. She had yet to learn what David Whyte writes in his poem "Sweet Darkness:"

You must learn one thing.
The world was made to be free in.[1]

This is the freedom to be who we are at a deep and soulful level. Our lives have purity and purpose that go deeper and flow more truly than any of our abilities to dam(n) or pollute them.

Various as trickling creeks, thundering waves, granite-carving glaciers, or still mountain pools, our deepest desires shape the topography of our lives. And this you can trust: our true longings are an expression of eternal surges deep within our souls; they cannot be destroyed.

Dive in. See how the water holds you. Let it carry you to the heart of your being and into a life that's beyond anything you've imagined.

It is time to find your river and ride it home.

CHAPTER 13

Originality

What river has no source?

–Jorge Luis Borges

Upriver for weeks and even months, sometimes for hundreds of miles, they swim. Over rapids, rocks, boulders, waterfalls, and logs, they struggle to the place of their birth to spawn. This is a pilgrimage both ancient and heroic.

Just as the salmon make their journey upstream, so there may come a time when we, too, desire to return to the source of who we are. The salmon teach us that this is no ordinary journey. Simple steps won't help to reunite us with our original self.

How do we find our way back?

I have been waiting all winter for the rains to fall hard enough and the tides to rise high enough to breach the sandbank on Muir Beach and open the gate for the coho to return from the Pacific, home to Redwood Creek to spawn. Only a few now make the migration, their bodies silver-muscled, ocean-fed, thrashing upstream like leaping light, swaying back and forth in their efforts to fight the currents.

As their tails slap and splash against the swollen waters, I watch in awe, wrapped against the cold and towered over by giant redwoods that cast shadows across the stream.

The poetry of these salmons' lives is written in river water. It was from this river that they swam downstream, plunged into the salty ocean, traveled on snaking currents over many moons and miles. And it is to this river that they are returning. Do they navigate by scent? Or perhaps the pull of electromagnetic fields irresistibly draws them back. No one really knows. Their homeward migration is one of the most wild and mysterious events that happens in nature.

Flow, river, origin. The salmon's struggle teaches me we aren't always supposed to ride the current outward; sometimes we need to travel against the current and work our way upstream. Isn't this the classic story of the heroic return, a pilgrimage in reverse?

It's as if one night under a chill moon you awake and know that you are lost. And with every water cell of your body, you long to find yourself again. The outward journey may be perilous, but the call to return is more challenging still. For the salmon, the pull is an impulse woven into the fabric of their being; but for you, the journey will have to be made consciously, born of a desire to discover the source of who you truly are. There will be many challenges. Yet something in the soul strives and leaps—all flash, and fin, and faith—toward a genuine life.

You might think that knowing who you are is a given. Yet it seems we each come into this world with a mission that we forget at the instant of our birth. Our lives are strewn with clues, but the fast-pulsing forward motion of existence carries us along so swiftly, we often don't have time to contemplate where we are headed or why we are here.

The Danish philosopher Søren Kierkegaard believed that though life must be lived forward, it can only be understood by looking backward. You need to make time to find the strong current of your story and track it to its source.

I sit by Redwood Creek, my ears straining to listen for the distant hum of the stream's beginning, where it starts on the slopes of Mount Tamalpais. River stones gleam in the churned waters, looking like an ancient road to a forgotten world. I take out my journal, inhale the mossy air, and begin an exercise called Steppingstones to record the significant events that mark the flow of my life.*

I slow my breath and release my thoughts to return upstream. Memories and images emerge, standing out like rocks in the river. I describe these with short phrases: "Escaping my crib," "Dancing by moonlight," "Climbing Mount Shasta." One memory captures my attention above the others. I am three years old, dancing naked on the lawn of my grandparents' home in North Yorkshire. I am round and dimpled, delirious with joy, free as the clouds in the sky, free as the creek that flows in this moment before me.

In our journey home, certain memories can act like magnets calling us back to ourselves. Some we will welcome; others will prove profoundly painful. Dams impede all but 1 percent of North American rivers, not only affecting the outgoing flow but the ability of the salmon to return to their birthplace. Our harrowing recollections can act as dams as well. Already straining against the current, we may experience these memories as insurmountable blocks. And yet, when we meet them without judgment, labeling them neither good nor bad, we open the way to return.

It seems ironic, but it is remarkably true that to fully inhabit our lives, we first need to spiritually and psychologically leave our "Mother River." We need to lose ourselves in all kinds of experiences—even suffer heartbreak or mislay the thread of our story—before we can return to discover the beauty of our true natures, who we really are.

It turns out the gift of our originality isn't handed to us at the headwaters of our journey, but granted when we find the courage to confront all the impediments that stand in our way. And nothing in our experience is wasted.

The returning salmon carry the richness of the great ocean within them in nutrients that nourish the birds of prey and other creatures of their community. Later, their bones will fertilize the soil and plants within their watershed. So you, in returning to your source, bring to your community the gift of all you have lived and learned.

---

* Steppingstones, developed by Ira Progoff as part of his Intensive Journal Process, is a means of reflecting on the "course that our life has taken from its beginning to the present moment."

Redwood Creek has a music all its own. As does each river. As does each person. Out at sea the salmon hear the song of their bloodstream calling to them. How and why this happens remains a mystery. As we grapple with the mystery of what it is to be human—both distinctly original and participating in the whole river of life—we are also called back to our source.

Find your river. Follow the story to your beginning.

It is time to make your way back.

Originality Exploration

If you live close to a river or creek, head there for this exploration. If that's not possible, simply find a quiet place in nature (or in the comfort of your living room) to spend an hour or two.

As you cast your energy and imagination back upstream (literally and/or metaphorically), allow memories to surface of when you felt most at home in your own skin and the world. Make a list of no more than ten steppingstones, describing them in short phrases. For example, walking with friends to school . . . playing the flute . . . my first swim. When you're done, arrange your list in chronological order.

Each small steppingstone holds worlds of information about who you are. Together, they point to patterns and aspects of your own true nature.

Choose one that calls to you right now. Then allow a stream of memories to flow toward you. Invite them in, body, mind, and soul.

Progoff recommends starting your journal-write with the phrase, *It was a time when. . .* to help you write about one of the moments or events on your steppingstones list.

For example, I wrote:

It was a time when I was the dancing child, round and tubby, with spongy feet on green grass. I was comfortable in my naked skin. I loved the spray of water from the hose, the rainbows it created, the great arc of the sky with its puffy clouds above me. My grandparents and parents delighted in me. I was the child of smiles and dancing legs. I knew the rhythm of my own soul. In Yorkshire, away from London, I was the dancing girl.

Reflecting back, I saw ways that little girl still comes out in me at times. She reminds me of the playful sensuousness of life. More than that, she carries the courage and confidence I need to feel when I'm writing or teaching about the wild soul.

When you reflect back on what you wrote, what do you discover?

CHAPTER 14

Depth

In the ocean said the oceanographer
there is no place to hide . . .

–Alicia Suskin Ostriker

For two years, my husband and I lived on the shores of Lake Pend Oreille in northern Idaho. The lake is one of the largest in America and so deep—more than a thousand feet in places—it was used to test submarines during World War II. Ruffled by light and motion, the lake sparkled. It was as if ten thousand white-winged birds fluttered across the surface.

On occasion as I swam out from land, a cloud passed overhead, the wind stilled, and the lake spread before me, inky black and menacing. I wondered what lay beneath, how deep the water was below me, what lived there. I shivered, recalling the myths of the great Pend Oreille water monster, and hurried back to shore.

We live on a blue planet. Earth holds 326 million cubic miles of water and all but 3 percent of this is stored in our oceans. These oceans form the largest area in the Universe known to be inhabited by living creatures. We have barely begun to explore their depths.

We skim the surface of our own consciousness as well, while the vast waters of our unconscious, the largest and most powerful part of us, remain invisible below. As I once heard Peter Russell, a leading thinker on consciousness, say, "We know more about the space outside than inside. We have so much to learn." The mystic Thomas Merton likewise asks, "What can we gain by sailing to the moon if we are not able to cross the abyss that separates us from ourselves?"[1]

Yet how many of us are willing to be deep-sea divers of our own souls?

More than ever, the glow of our electronic screens, like light on water, keeps us transfixed. Life moves so fast, is so scintillating, who has time to take the deep dive? It is toward depth, truth, and meaning that our souls yearn, however. Even as we glide along on the swift current of life, attempting to hold the depths at bay, we sense them calling to us. What marvels and mysteries might they hold?

The Mariana Trench in the Pacific Ocean is the deepest sea canyon on Earth, plunging at its lowest point to a staggering 36,201 feet. At its bottom is a world nearly unfathomable to the human mind. Imagine a canyon so deep it could swallow Mount Everest whole with a mile to spare. Imagine a place of intense darkness, freezing temperatures, and immense pressure. Now imagine that life exists even in this abyss—because it does.

The depths of the world's oceans are filled with strange and mystical beings uniquely adapted to life under pressure. In places so remote we thought there would be no life at all, the biodiversity can exceed that found in Earth's rainforests. More surprising still, we discover that many of these creatures of darkness are actually creatures of light.

Beyond the reach of the sun's rays, a fire-shooter shrimp releases self-created luminescence like a galaxy of stars into the ocean night; golden corals glow when something brushes against them, a starfish twinkles like diamonds; spirals and cords of light create a dazzling fireworks display. In the deepest and darkest places, living beings make their own light.

The soul knows that depth is what we need, however much we may try to avoid it. Yet finding the courage to fathom the ocean of our unconscious rarely happens of its own accord. And so, every once in a while, something disturbs the surface waters. We become depressed or anxious, an uncomfortable memory emerges, we have a dream that demands our attention or a vision that we cannot ignore. These disturbances can range from mildly unsettling to powerfully disruptive, but they are always a call to a deeper and more soulful way of living.

One night as I sat in a London theater, the waves came crashing over my head. I had been sober for several years, and on the surface I looked good. I had even earned the nickname "Little Miss Sunshine" because of my smiley countenance and upbeat personality. Inside, however, I churned with anxiety. I wasn't working the steps of my recovery program and was doing everything possible to avoid dealing with my real issues. I wanted life to be sparkly and happy. Having given up drinking, didn't I deserve that?

But that night, amid the hum of a full auditorium, I felt some part of me leave my body, dragged down into a realm where the air blurred and I could barely breathe. I had entered an alternative universe. If I screamed, no one would hear me. If I ran, I would end up back where I started. Like Jonah, I had disappeared into the belly of the whale.

A second later, I snapped back into my body.

After that, I knew I couldn't continue as before. It wasn't just my sobriety at risk but also my sanity. Thus began my own deep dive, taken with a series of sponsors and therapists who helped me uncover the painful patterns of my past. At first, I was terrified to enter the depths; I descended slowly and cautiously. Light rarely penetrates below 656 feet in the oceans. There were days when I felt crushed by the darkness and the pressure.

I recall scuba diving for the first time in Cancun, Mexico. Murky, weird, and gloaming at only thirty feet down, it was a different world. I had been instructed to stay close to my fellow divers and to breathe normally despite the claustrophobia I felt. I began to sink, descending deeper than I wanted. The light seemed so far away. Would I keep sinking? Would I ever be able to make it back to the surface again?

In braving my internal depths, I confronted challenges as well. What I discovered often shattered the illusion of who I believed myself to be. I stared into the abyss of my selfishness and self-will, the sexual messes of my younger years, and the devastating lack of self-esteem that had fueled so many of my wrong-headed decisions. I had to come up for air often before taking the next dive. And yet, miraculously, I also found that beauty and light aren't just attributes of life on the surface.

Alone in the depths, confronting the submerged and disowned aspects of myself, I rediscovered my passion, purpose, and playfulness. The light returned to my soul, at first in tiny glints and then great starbursts of pure joy. On the third time I scuba dived, I began to feel at home underwater. Just so, I have found myself able to enter my own depths more freely. With each descent, I become less dependent on seeking the source of light only in shiny objects and superficial things: the greater brilliance now glows from within.

Depth Exploration

Keeping a dream journal is a powerful way to begin exploring your depths.

As you prepare to go to sleep, fill a bowl with water and place a lit floating candle on its surface. As you watch the play of light on the water, breathe deeply, relaxing your body and opening yourself up to welcome your dreams.

When you feel deeply relaxed, blow out the candle and head to bed, remembering to keep a small flashlight, your journal, and a pen by your side. As soon as you wake, focus on any images you can recall from your dream and begin writing what you remember. After you've recorded your dream as fully as you can, ask:

What is the emotional tone of the dream?

What is the most powerful image in the dream? How does this image impact me?

What connections can I make between my dream and my waking life?

Write down your responses.

CHAPTER 15
Flow

. . . catch the current and ride it like an animal . . .

–Linda Hogan

Years ago, I took a rafting trip down the Klamath River. On the last morning, the group talked in anxious voices about "*the rapids*"—the kind that could suck you into a sinkhole like a leaf down a drain and pummel you against sharp rocks. We were fast approaching Dragon's Tooth, the most challenging stretch of water. Led by experienced guides, the rest of the group was going down the river on rafts. I chose to take it solo, in a small kayak.

As the rapids approached, the sound was thunderous. Dazzling spumes tossed rainbows in the air, and the water churned and curdled in frothing pools around my tiny boat. Every muscle in my body clenched.

Perhaps I should tell you, I like to be in control. When you grow up in an alcoholic family, you learn to take care of things and not rely on others. I've had problems of trust going back as far as I can remember. So hurtling toward a sinkhole made me want to stick my oar in and scream, "Stop!" I was certain I'd be pulled under and drown. I was as close to pure terror as I had ever been.

It was at that moment the osprey appeared and cried out. It flew just above my left shoulder, so close I could almost feel the breath of its wings. I stopped listening to the roar of the rapids and gazed up at the bird instead. It followed me, never leaving my side. And with each cry, with each beat of its sharp-tipped feathers, my heart calmed, my body slackened, and I felt myself merge into the current that swept me, weightless as a matchstick, through the churning waters.

I have no memory of whether I paddled or simply gave myself over to the river. What I do know was this: a dam had burst inside me. I was carried by a wild energy: part surrender, part liberation. It was more freeing than anything I had yet experienced

Later that night, lying beside the river under an August sky streaming with meteors, I reflected on how powerful it was to be carried along by something greater than myself. I had been sober for about six years at that time but had never handed the direction of my life over to a Higher Power, as I'd been encouraged to do. I was still manager—of myself, and just about everything and everyone around me. But that day, I had a visceral feeling of finally letting go.

I thought about rivers starting as a trickle, high in hills or mountains, and gathering force as they descend, swelling into streams, feeding off tributaries, getting broader and bigger. I wondered if faith didn't grow this way too: slight and slow and then deepening and widening with time. And what it would take for my faith to truly flow?

We live in a world that dominates nature, and this leads us to dominate as a habit—other people, and worse still, our own spirits. As one of my students wrote, "I am weary of all the internal rules of how I 'should' be that disconnect me from the wild flow within."

Perhaps faith is nothing more than embracing the wild flow that courses within each of us. In catching sight of the osprey that day, I felt as if Spirit had arrived to remind me that I was always being looked after—that it would be okay to surrender to the current.

In 1935, sixty million tons of concrete were laid to create Hoover Dam (so much concrete it is still curing). At some point in our lives, we began to pour concrete of our own. It was made of anxiety, fear, and stress. Our task is to bring down the walls of our own inner dams. We can learn to dismantle them. And we can begin by asking ourselves what kind of lives we want. Do we want to micromanage every moment, or do we want to dismantle our control and trust the great river to carry us forward?

An untamed river, after all, is alive. It erodes banks and bursts them; it seeks new courses. It floods, and is astonishingly powerful. Dammed water is monumentally static: trapped, regulated, stagnant. Do we want to live in faith or do we want to be held back by fear?

When I'm in the flow—writing, hiking, making love with my husband—I know these are the most ecstatic times of my life. These are the times of my great self-forgetting, when the ego drops away and my anxiety with it. I become a channel for something wonderful to flow through me . . . creativity, celebration, love.

In these moments the breath of spirit, like the osprey at my shoulder, reminds me to let go and ride the wild river into the heart of my life.

Who would you be if you were free?

Flow Exploration

On a hot day, take yourself to a swimming pool, a lake, or the ocean. Or at any time, fill the bathtub and relax back into the water. Let it carry you. Trust your body to the water and feel yourself held. The more you relax, the more the water will hold you.

As you lie there, recognize that you are floating on the planet with nothing to hold you but gravity; that the planet is cradling you with just the right amount of force. You do not feel constrained, but neither are you abandoned. Trust is built. You know that you are safe, held up by water, held close by gravity, looking up at the immensity of an infinite Universe.

Next time you're in the water, remember how much your body trusts to the laws of this finely tuned cosmos. Let it be a reminder to you that just as surely, you can trust Spirit to guide and carry you through life.

When you're ready, spend a few minutes writing a response to the question "Who would I be—what would I do—if I trusted that I was carried by Spirit?"

CHAPTER 16

Expressiveness

It's hard to be water . . .

–Brenda Hillman

Think of me—river water, deep flowing, silver-backed, slipping through canyons, tumbling into pools of green, over rough-skinned rocks, between roots of trees. Think of me in spring, thundering over the lip of the world. Or when I am slow, sludge heavy, short of breath. When rain pummels my back like sharp pins, and I bloat and breach my banks. When the sun rises and turns black ink to gold, and night falls and I hold a sky of stars. Think of me, through industrial cities dark with poison, a repository of filth and chemicals, as my body cries out with pain. As I shimmer in a meadow, a ribbon of light in a sea of grass. Think of me, as I journey from glacier, down mountainside and scarred slopes, into wells deep in the Earth where I pool, warmed by fire. As I shape-shift from steam to ice, raindrop to snow crystal, spill into oceans and rise as mist above rainforests. Think of me flowing through your veins, dripping into every crest and valley of your being.

For whenever you think of me, in whatever form, I am always the same river.[1]

–Journal entry, August 13, 2011

Water reminds us that we are able to show up in alternate ways and forms without abandoning our true nature. We are shape-shifters. Depending on the environment and circumstances and our own internal state, we may express as thunderous anger, icy disdain, or a bubbling brook of joy.

Contemporary social mores tend to tamp down authentic and spontaneous expression. We have been programmed to react like clockwork, calculate and calibrate our feelings, in order to comply with a mechanistic, industrialized system that values efficiency over feelings. And yet, our power lies in our passions. We can be flooded with emotion in any moment. The waters of our sacred being are not easily controlled.

My friend Mary Jo discovered this at seven years sober. The anger she experienced was so intense, people worried for her. She told me, "I felt homicidal, as if every nerve ending was on fire. Rage poured through me." Her therapist defied common wisdom and supported her in forgoing medication. She believed Mary Jo's rage was a rite of passage necessary to healing from the painful wounds of her past. For seven months, during her seventh year of sobriety, Mary Jo was by self-account a madwoman: wild, raging, steaming. Like Mrs. Rochester in the attic; like Kali; like the Greco-Roman Furies, goddesses of vengeance and daughters of Gaea. Her blood boiled. But the poisons moved out of her, and when she was done she felt as if a part of her that had been frozen had finally broken free.

Living close to our hearts is not about being perfect. Water reminds us that there will be times when in order to heal, we will need to express our rage, our pain, our hurt. There will be other times when we need to call upon the slow strength of glaciers, or act like the gentlest rain or an unstoppable torrent, or draw on the still, calm waters of our innermost beings.

In the words of the poet Langston Hughes, our souls have "grown deep like the rivers."[2] When we embrace and express the fullness of our soulful emotions, we begin to discover the deep current of love that runs within us. Owning our passions, we connect to our unstoppable hearts. Our emotions become cleaner and clearer. They flow from deep within and in genuine response to our present circumstances.

Water, ice, steam. Our true powers of expression come from knowing the many forms of our own river.

Expressiveness Exploration

Make a list all the forms water takes, from icebergs to waterfalls. Which forms seem to most resemble your emotional landscape? Once you identify the range of forms your feelings take, seek their exemplars, either directly in nature, or in images of water in magazines or videos. As you contemplate these different permutations of water, consider how they reflect your own gamut of emotions, and record your observations in your journal.

Next, recall a situation that caused an emotional response. Write about the situation in the present tense, and describe the quality of the emotions evoked in you in terms of water images. As you reflect back on what you've written, ask yourself these questions:

What have I learned about the states my emotions appear in?

Could I have expressed my feelings in a more genuine way?

Would greater emotional honesty have created a more optimal outcome or allowed for more healing or growth?

Complete this exploration by making a collage or vision board with representations of both your current and desired forms of expressions.

CHAPTER 17

Ebb and Flow

There is something infinitely healing in the repeated refrains of nature.

–Rachel Carson

The tide is out this morning in the estuary.

Tussocks of grass spring from water thin as a windowpane. A plover picks his way in the shallows, and sandpipers flit like tossed pebbles from one channel to another. Closer in, a Canada goose imprints the muddy bank. A great egret floats by on white handkerchief wings, her hoarse croak rending the quiet air.

In the afternoon, the tide turns, drowning the grasses, dispersing the waders, causing currents to snake and swirl. Ducks float by like bunches of water lilies. The current, landward facing, rushes in from the Pacific. Later the tide will shift again and the sea will call her salty body home.

And don't the seasons also turn; doesn't night follow day? Doesn't your own soul long to ebb and flow—not to the tempo of the modern world's frantic beat, but according to its own internal rhythm?

Ebb and Flow Exploration

Meditate on how the moon waxes and wanes, tides ebb and flow, and seasons shift and cycle. Feel how your own soul follows a similar pattern. Do you welcome this flux of energy as natural? Or do you fight it?

What might it be like if you simply followed your own internal rhythm?

As you attune to nature's cadences, see if you can discern which ones will most sustain you. You might choose a particular spot in nature and visit it at different times throughout the year, to meditate on the flux and flow of life.

After meditating, take out your journal and begin writing:

"The sustaining rhythm for my life right now would be . . ."

Note: As you return to this exploration again and again, you will find that your life begs a different tempo at different times and stages.

CHAPTER 18

Desire

Don't say, don't say there is no water.

–Denise Levertov

My mother corners me while I take my bath to give me sex education. She tells me that when I meet a boy I like, I will become wet—"down there."

My blood runs. I run, to the bathroom, from the dormitory of my Catholic English boarding school. Mother Monk tells me off for making such a fuss.

I kiss my first boy, body close, tongue wet. My mother was right.

I make love, taste semen, salty as the oceans. In free flow, I drift from boy to boy, drowning. I am drawn to cross the Atlantic to live in New York, leave to make my home by the Pacific Ocean, learn to make love sober.

I experience one ectopic pregnancy, and then another. My womb will not fill. Later, I will dream I am swimming underwater looking for a lost kitten.

I will have a partial hysterectomy. One ovary will survive. My body will begin to dry up.

I will marry a man whose kisses keep me moist. Channels of desire, well worn, will recede. New ones will open up. Poems will flow. I will sit in the sun and melt like spring snow. My pen will drip words.

I will long, with all that is in me, to find the pure current—the water that is safe to drink. I will look ahead to the time when the water evaporates.

I will remember the rightness of my mother's words:
Desire and water are one.

–Journal entry, October 11, 2012

Desire Exploration

Now it is your turn to write your biography of desire as told through water.

Take a few deep breaths, sense into your own watery body, and reflect back on your relationship with desire. I encourage you to capture your story in short sentences and bold images. Allow the words to flow freely, and without too much forethought or control.

Where did desire start for you? What causes it to keep flowing? What causes it to dry up? How skillful are you at riding the currents of desire?

After you've completed your biography of desire, take some time to reflect on it. What do you notice?

Now it is time to write out your "desired vision" for desire in your life.

What would it look like?

How and where would it flow through the landscape of your life?

What would be possible for you and your life if it flowed more naturally and more passionately?

Record your responses in your journal.

Chapter 19
Balance

When creeks are full
The poems flow
When creeks are down
We heap stones.

–Gary Snyder

There was a drought in a village in China. They sent for a rainmaker who lived far away. He arrived to find the village in a sorry state: cattle dying, vegetation shriveled, people thirsty. The villagers crowded around him asking what he planned to do. He responded, "Give me a hut and leave me alone for a few days."

He disappeared into the hut. For two days, nothing happened. On the third day it started to pour. When the rainmaker came out of the hut, the villagers were eager to know what he'd done. "That is very simple, " he said. "I didn't do anything."

"But it is raining," they said.

"I come from the area of Tao, in balance," he explained. "We have rain—we have sunshine. Nothing is out of order. In your area everything is chaotic. The rhythm of life is disturbed, so I, too, am disturbed. So what can I do? I went into the hut to be by myself, to meditate, to set myself straight.

"When I get myself in order, everything around is set right. We are now in Tao. Now it rains."

This was one of Carl Jung's favorite stories.[1]

76

I have my own favorite story of how balance and flow can be restored, told to me by one of my workshop participants. This is Lonner Holden's story:

"Twelve years ago my wife had cancer. Our children were young at the time, and my wife was unable to work as she went through chemo and concentrated on healing. For two years I was the sole breadwinner, caretaker, and single parent."

Consumed by intense demands, Lonner thought only about holding things together. When his wife was well enough to go back to work and life began to assume the old routine, Lonner caught his reflection in the bathroom mirror one morning. As he put it, "I couldn't seem to see myself. Somewhere in all this stress and work, I had vanished. There was nothing left of me."

At the same time a friend called to tell Lonner that there had been a cancellation on a rafting trip down the Colorado River. Did Lonner want to come? Despite all the arguments against going—responsibilities, cost, work—Lonner's body cried out "Yes." He knew this nine-day river trip was a lifeline.

The vast walls of the Grand Canyon towered over him, carrying life in every tiny particle of shining sand and rock. "And for the first time in so long I wasn't having to do the carrying—the river was carrying me. Without knowing it, my soul was being massaged into a deep state of rest and release.

"On the final morning, we were thrust quietly and smoothly out of the canyon into the opening of the lake. It was a true spiritual birthing for me. Few moments in my life have been so suddenly transforming. Nine days of gestation culminating in a single dramatic moment of coming around the bend into space, light, and self-acceptance. The Colorado's gift had been of me."

After listening to the story of Lonner's sacred journey, I walked outside into a cold January night. In the aftermath of a heavy rainstorm, water gushed over gutters and streamed down hillsides. I stood there, considering the peculiar way we humans have come to think of ourselves as separate from nature, and how in doing so, we are tipping the balance. We are exhausting the Earth by the demands we put on her. We are draining ourselves too, sapping the flow of vitality though constant stress and overwork, and our push for more, more, more.

What would it take to get our own internal house in order?

In the cool night air, I exhaled deeply, sending a tiny puff of cloud out into the world to become raindrop, snowflake, river.

When the creeks are full, the river of life can flow.

Balance Exploration

Take a clear glass and fill it half full. Take a moment to reflect on the water in the glass, perhaps lighting a candle or setting the glass by a window where sunlight will play on the water. As you contemplate the glass and water, bring out your journal and reflect on these two questions:

How is my life empty?

How is my life full?

Then ask:

What could I release to allow for more balance in my life?

What could I give myself to allow for more balance in my life?

When you are done, drink the water, giving thanks for this life-giving element.

CHAPTER 20
Generosity

. . . all things flow back to the sea from which they came.

–Rabbi George Gittleman

Within each of our cells is a miniscule sea. The water molecules inside us arose from all the oceans of the world; they evaporated from rainforests, settled as snow on mountaintops, and coursed through rivers. More than 70 percent of the Earth's surface is ocean, and our bodies carry a similar ratio of salt water to flesh and bone.

Immense, generative, and generous, the ocean is the womb from which all life emerged. Oceans give life and—in the form of violent waves, deadly currents, and towering tsunamis—have the power to take it back.

For me, water has always been a magnet. I love to feel released from my own weight, gently held, buoyant. As a wayward teenager and beyond, I sneaked into hotel and backyard pools. Even today, the need to immerse myself in water is so strong that my body aches to leave the land. The sight of a certain color blue makes me crave water, long to stretch out, slide sleek and weightless in its arms.

Whether the Mediterranean Sea of my childhood, or the Pacific just minutes from where I now live, the ocean has always helped me to feel reborn.

On a stormy December weekend in 1983, I was hiking along the exposed bluffs of the Marin Headlands north of the Golden Gate Bridge. I'd quit drinking just days before, and was shaky and afraid. I had no idea if I could live without alcohol. From the bluff, I gazed across a mad motion of dance and fury. The ocean mirrored my inner turmoil. It also calmed me. I sensed an invitation to see my own inner churning not as a sign of weakness but in light of my own gathering strength. I tasted salt. I didn't know if it was the ocean's or mine. I felt completely at one with this immense body of water. In some unnameable way, I knew I was going to be all right.

According to underwater explorer Jacques Cousteau, each of the twenty-eight bones of the human skull can be traced back to the bony part in the head of a prehistoric fish. The same tidal surges that move fish and stir the ocean tug at our bodies too. On a full moon night we toss, restless in our beds, caught in the rising tides of our swelling emotions.

But we are severing this intricate connection.

In their grand generosity the oceans are sacrificing themselves for us. Absorbing more and more of the carbon dioxide we pump into the atmosphere, seawater is becoming so acidic that it is dissolving and eating away the shells of small shell creatures like crabs, oysters, and krill (the major food sources for fish like salmon, herring, and mackerel). Coral reefs are bleaching and dying. Like the good mother she is, the ocean is taking the heat, quite literally, for global warming.

How have we managed to lose such regard for our great mothering ocean? How have we forgotten our debt to her and our deep kinship with her? "The ocean refuses no river, no matter where that river has been or what it might have picked up on its journey," writes the activist Ocean Robbins.[1] When we pollute our oceans, the toxins find their way back into our tears and our human mothers' amniotic fluid. How can we revere rather than destroy the elemental entity that gave birth to *us*?

The ocean's great and generative spirit is embedded within the immensity of our souls. We see this in how drawn we are to her. We rush to her side, play in her foamy skirts, rest upon her skin. But still we can neglect what she is to us. In this deep forgetting, we lose sight of our rightful relationship to the ocean. And our own powers become distorted and dangerous.

I don't know what God is, but I am struck time and again by a phrase used by the renowned religious expert Huston Smith. He is very old and frail now, and when I first saw him he was poised like an ancient King Neptune on his throne. When asked why he was convinced of the presence of God, he replied, "Because all of my life I've experienced oceans of goodness."[2]

Contemplating the ocean, we are in the presence of a raw power that can teach us how to wield our own power judiciously and generously. The ocean can unleash incredible forces of destruction, but its waters, its depths, are ultimately life giving. How can we employ our immense capacities as human beings to be equally generative?

As I look out at the Pacific now, a song of salt again rushes toward me on the wind. I listen to its whisper, and it tells me that we are generous, creative, life-giving beings. But we also have the ability to destroy.

The choice is ours.

Generosity Exploration

Find a quiet spot and let go of any distracting thoughts. As your breath settles into a steady rhythm, you will find yourself entering a calm, meditative state. Next, put your hand to your heart, or gently feel for the pulse in your wrist. Listen to the individual song of your heart, filled with its particular longings and love.

When you are ready, rest your hands in your lap and simply sense into the ocean of spirit that lives in your depths. Feel its power and its beauty. It holds the potential for so much generosity as well as incredible destruction.

What will you choose?

How will you know you have chosen it?

What is the gift you are longing to give from this deep place?

Record your answers in your journal.

∽ Leaving the Oceans and Rivers ∽

This soulscape invites us to explore our deepest longings and urges. Was it a natural place for you to dive in and play? Or did it feel overwhelming? How was your experience?

As you leave this soulscape, reflect upon what currents are pulling at you. You may find yourself longing to surrender to some while resisting others. Some aspects may still feel too frightening to explore.

Don't judge your reactions; simply allow yourself to become curious as you delve more deeply into what the oceans and rivers have to offer you in the way of wisdom.

What have you learned about your own powerful longings and desires?

What more do you long to know? Or be?

Right now, allow any particularly strong insights you have gleaned to float to the surface so you can capture them in your journal.

Part 4
Mountains

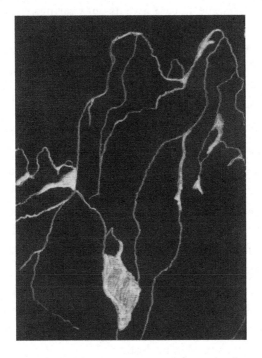

*I will speak to you in mountain language,
answer with the strength of stone.*

. . . there is no upness comparable to the mountains.

–John Muir

They soar to snowcapped peaks and slice the sky. In sunlight they recall the spiritual grace of cathedrals. Gods of the planet, mountains rise to touch the heavens. They shape the landscape, affect weather, form boundaries between countries, and influence the flow of water. They are anchors and icons and sacred places. Visible from miles around, the highest peaks give us our bearings.

Known by many names—the Himalayas, the Rockies, the Karakoram, the Tien Shan—mountains carve out space in our psyches. In Ancient Greece, the great god Zeus, who ruled Mount Olympus, spawned nearly a hundred mountain cults; Chinese sacred mountains are powerful sites of telluric power; for Native Americans who live on or near majestic mountains, these places are holy. Homes to dragons and deities, mountains thrill us, frighten us, inspire us.

Mountains speak to the power that is within us to shape our world according to what we truly value. Without mountains the Earth would flatten into endless monotony. Without the need to aspire to great heights, our lives would be equally dull. Imagine a world in which you never reached for a vision. Imagine a world without dreams.

When we seek our full aliveness, we make the mountains our home. For life in the mountains is a grand adventure. Filled with risks, challenges, and even setbacks and sacrifices, the mountains give our lives a heroic edge. Here, we thrive under pressure; we are not afraid of being seen or known, of claiming our destiny.

Mountains are formed in many ways—from volcanic uprisings or collisions of land plates to steady carving by glaciers—and so what brings us to the mountains may also differ dramatically. We may be roused by anger, slowly shaped by outside forces, or, like Heidi Kühn, a woman I met at a small gathering of Earth-conscious activists, we may find our lives colliding with the one thing that will reshape the entire landscape of our existence.

Heidi described it to me this way: When Princess Diana died and she learned of her work with landmines, something inside Heidi broke open. She knew right away that she *had* to do something. Heidi went on to found Roots of Peace, with the idea of swapping mines for vines, turning "dead" land in Afghanistan into verdant, peaceful orchards. This wasn't what Heidi had planned, but when destiny called she willingly stepped up. Today, Roots of Peace is working in numerous countries including Cambodia, Iraq, and Afghanistan, where they recently planted fifteen thousand trees in Kabul.

Yet many resist the mountains' call. We know we're supposed to write that book or give up the cozy career for one with meaning. One client, a corporate consultant, succumbed to vertigo when asked to step into her spiritual calling. Whenever she thought of taking her spiritual beliefs into the workplace, she found herself sick and dizzy, forced back into bed. She experienced her fear of heightened exposure as a whirling loss of balance, as if looking down from a great height.

The taller the mountain range, the thicker the Earth's crust needed to support it. In order to give rise to our fullness, we must be strong in our being. Those who get rocketed to fame without a solid foundation to build upon often find themselves self-destructing. We may need to defer our ascent until we feel an inner fortitude or have created a robust support system around us. Or we may know in our hearts that it is time.

Whatever the case, the quest begins humbly, from right where we are. We move toward something we wish to accomplish or achieve. We step up. We show up. We see what we are made of. The vision grows, and we hear another call. We step up again and again, reach for higher peaks, still greater visions. This process builds our spiritual muscles.

When we assume the strength of the mountain, we grow in authenticity; we have a greater impact on the world. When we stay the course, we eventually confront our own personal Everest—our ultimate aliveness—the mountain of all mountains. In this steep place, on these treacherous slopes, even the gods are brought to their knees. But if we make it to the peak, we will soar.

At the summit, we spread our arms wide. We fly. We see the world from a fresh perspective—one that is denied us if we don't embrace the risks and challenges of the climb. This is the "Inspiration Point" of our being. Here, we know we are on the planet for a purpose; we see that everything in our lives has conspired to bring us to this place: at once liberated and belonging.

CHAPTER 21

Solidity

*Go inside a stone
That would be my way.*

–Charles Simic

Lame Deer, the Sioux medicine man, said, "Every man needs a stone to help him . . . Deep inside you there must be an awareness of the rock power, of the spirits in them, otherwise you would not pick them up and fondle them as you do."[1]

What is it that we touch when we touch a stone? What is it that we seek? Is it our own weight or substance? Do we feel, in the smooth granite against our thumbs, the grain and grit we contain? Mountains and rocks are the bones of the Earth. Are we trying to reach the bones of who we are—that place of "rock power" that resides in us?

On southeast Brittany's Morbihan coast one blistering hot day in August, I visited the Carnac Stones. More than three thousand ancient standing stones, laid out in varied alignments, shimmered across the scorched landscape. Some were arranged like squat houses, others slim and tall as trees. Where prehistoric people once lived, many megalithic sites like this one, and others like Stonehenge, still remain.

The incredible work of hewing and moving all that rock, the myriad helpers, the sweat and sacrifice involved in creating these sacred places is almost impossible to grasp. The result is a powerful dance of substance and shadow, starlight and solstices. These "spirit" stones connect us to the great spinning cosmos—the realm of the gods.

Even today, many who take my workshops talk of being stone collectors. One woman, Kristin, described a rock she spotted at the side of the road while bicycling. It so captured her attention that she stopped in her tracks, later returning in her car to take the rock back home to form the cornerstone of her fire pit.

She wrote: "I thought about how the rock may have traveled many miles to where it ended up in the ditch, and of making a place for it in my outside hearth, soaking in the rain, the sun, the moonlight, and the occasional heat from the fire's flame. I was reminded of my father and sat with those memories for some time. I pondered how my dad was always *my rock*, my mountain—larger than life in his six feet six frame. I felt healing support through this rock."

In October 1989, the Earth rose and fell, ocean waves beneath my feet. A 7.1 magnitude earthquake shook San Francisco and tossed me about like a rag doll. Standing on the fourth floor of the old Phelan Building downtown, I experienced the terror of the absence of terra firma as walls cracked, windows shattered, and the ground buckled. For years afterward, the slightest tremble would leave me breathless with panic.

When the damage from the earthquake was assessed, it was those buildings built on solid rock that survived the best.

"Words and paper . . . did not seem real enough to me . . . I had to make a confession of faith in stone," wrote Carl Jung as he began work on the stone tower at his home in Bollingen on the upper lake in Zurich.[2] Jesus proclaimed, "Upon this rock I will build my church." Bedrock is the solid rock that underpins the shifting soils. It is the foundation on which we feel secure in building everything from churches to the intricacies of our fleeting lives. Resting upon bedrock, we sleep soundly.

Pondering this, I consider the horrific practice of fracking, a means of natural oil or gas extraction that injects gallons of slurry at incredibly high pressure into rock, shattering it, creating fissures miles beneath Earth's surface. The Earth trembles under the assault. Earthquakes follow, even in normally stable areas. And don't our psyches sometimes shatter under undue pressure as well? And don't we find ourselves looking for that strong and solid place beneath all the brokenness and the hurt? We have to believe that deep inside of us there is something untouchable—unbreakable.

I think of a story about a young man called Gregory, told to me by Susan, who volunteers to care for the mentally ill. A borderline schizophrenic, Gregory was afraid of pointed-toed shoes. In Susan's words, "He walked backward. To go forward, he crawled. He was frightened of most everything."

One Saturday, Susan and Gregory were sitting down together in a quadrangle at the University of Illinois, surrounded by red brick buildings. Construction had left a huge pile of small stones in one corner of the yard.

"Look at all the colors," blurted Gregory, pointing to the stone pile and staring at it—without averting his eyes, as he usually did. He appeared transfixed. Susan looked at the stone pile. "Colors?" she thought.

Then, as Susan described it, "Gregory began to crawl toward the stone pile, taking one handful of stones and then another. Then slowly, he stood up—a tall, tall mountain of a boy, with pockets full of stones."

Together, they walked home.

Solidity Exploration

Native Americans made a medicine pouch into which they placed ancestor stones. These stones were their guides because they possessed ancient knowledge.

Create your own medicine pouch from a small bag or purse. Choose a bag (or make one) that feels intuitively right to you. Choose five to ten stones, using your same intuitive skills. Place them in your hand, admiring their shape and smoothness, their texture and color. Only if the stone feels just right does it belong in your pouch.

Once you've chosen your stones, write about each of them in your journal. Describe their shape, texture, size, how they feel in your hand.

Who are these stones?

What energy do they carry?

What knowledge do they hold?

What wisdom can they offer about what is enduring and indestructible within you?

How do you feel when you have them with you?

Explore these questions in your journal.

CHAPTER 22

Extremity

I have this mountain to climb
and no one to stop me . . .

–David Ignatow

Towering and massive, mountains may rise many thousands of feet above the safe skirts of the tree line. Here, the winds and the elements strike hard, nothing standing in their way. If you want to get out of your comfort zone, climb a mountain. Mountaintops are exposed.

In 1995, I received a last-minute invitation from a friend to join a trekking party in the Himalayas. Before I could think of the practicalities, the cost, I'd said yes. On the outside, my actions might have appeared impulsive, even reckless. My bank account wasn't robust, nor was my boss delighted. But I saw it a different way. At almost forty, having just separated from my second husband and with no children to wrap me in respectability, I felt as if I was failing at life. I needed to shake things up.

I did worry about vertigo. Mine is the kind that makes me feel as if I'll be sucked into the void. If I'm on a ski lift that stalls, it takes all my self-control not to go crazy with fear. So while I've always loved mountains, I'd never really tested myself or ever been higher than eight thousand feet. I had no idea what awaited me in Nepal. I just hoped that the trails would be wide and that I wouldn't become paralyzed with panic.

What I hadn't anticipated was the weather, which was supposed to be summerlike in November.

The storm arrived on the fourth day of our trek when we were camped above fourteen thousand feet. Icy sleet like lead bullets pummeled my tent, and high winds sent neighboring tents scattering. Our group stayed huddled, visiting the nearby tea hut to stay warm and dry. After two days, the weather cleared. We awoke to a blue sky and sweeping views of the Annapurna Range, the snowcapped peaks pink in the early morning light. We could move on.

We'd camped just below the snowline, but now we were headed to above fifteen thousand feet. The slope was steep, snowbound, and slippery. At times, we struggled thigh deep in thick drifts. Stopping by a simple stone stupa, its prayer flags fluttering against a blazing sky, the news came—one of our porters had slid down the hillside and was seriously hurt. He would have to return home to his village. It slowly dawned on us that if we were to go on, we would quite literally be risking our lives.

JP, our Nepalese guide, left to check on the porter and see if he could get help. His only equipment was a black British umbrella with a curved wooden handle, which he used as a walking stick. We were completely unprepared for these extreme conditions. An hour later JP returned, bringing with him a German party equipped with ropes and crampons. They would break trail and help us cross the next section of mountain until we descended to Gosainkunda Lake below the snowline. In their cool glances we felt their disdain for our amateurism.

At first, it was relatively easy going. We fell into a steady rhythm; the only sound was the crunching of boots on snow. Then the line halted. In front of us was a quarter-mile stretch of staggeringly steep cliff with a drop of thousands of feet. The Germans would lead the way.

I was the last to cross except for the porters who trailed behind me. I stepped carefully, planting my feet in the footprints in front. Clouds swirled beneath me, some billowing yellow in the sunlight, and the sky was so blue it was almost black. Where the already slender trail narrowed further, the Germans fixed ropes, telling us that they could only be relied on to take the weight of two people at a time. I watched how the others navigated the stretch of about two hundred feet or so, turning inward, the length of their boots almost the exact width of the newly made trail. They held the ropes firmly in both hands; if their feet slipped, they might still hang on and be rescued.

I took off my gloves so I could better hold the ropes. Without lunch, and with wet, cold feet, I was already shaky and vulnerable to slipping. I breathed, praying to the mountain gods, and took my first step. The rope felt comfortable in my hands, seeming not just to anchor me physically but emotionally to the mountainside. By the time I was halfway across, I thought, *If I just keep calm, I'll make it.* That's when the rope pulled partly away from the rock.

I looked back. Three of our porters were frantically tugging at the rope, the full weight of their packs straining against the pitons that held the rope in place. If the rope were to continue to hold, I'd have to let go. I put my hands to the mountain face, my whole body as close to the body of the massive mountain as I could get. Each step was agonizingly slow, my body as tense as wire. Ravens called loudly, even at this height. I could feel the edge of the mountain at the heel of my boot. If I stepped back, my foot would find nothing—just the vast sky. How easy it would be to fly off the face of the Earth.

When I reached a wider section of the trail about fifteen minutes later, my whole body shook with adrenaline.

Later, below the snowline at Gosainkunda and giddy with relief, we regaled a group of British SAS, one of the toughest fighting units in the world, with our adventures. They were taking the same trek but in the opposite direction. "Cor Blimey!" one said. "We turned back—it looked too dangerous for us."

I left the group and headed outside. Above me, the Milky Way spilled an avalanche of stars across the black slope of night. I thought about why, even in this day and age of creature comforts, we humans still feel the need to risk ourselves on the mountains. Standing alone in the crystal clear night, I had no idea what would await me on my return home. I only knew that, like the ravens that had followed us all day, and in the words of the poet Rilke, I wanted to "live my life in widening circles / that reach out across the world."[1]

The mountain had pushed me past my limits. In ways I had yet to discover, my life was about to get larger.

Extremity Exploration

Have you ever taken a risk and stepped out of your comfort zone? What were your beliefs about the situation before you took the risk? What stories did you tell yourself about what would happen?

After stepping out of your comfort zone, what did you discover? What did you learn about yourself from risking yourself and stepping out on the edge?

As you contemplate your answers, write down a list of at least five risks you are ready to take now in your life. These can be anything from changing careers to giving a talk, speaking your truth, or taking on a physical challenge like hiking a mountain!

Then ask: "How will I feel when I've taken these risks?" Write about your experience from the perspective of having taken the risk.

Write your risk story in your journal.

CHAPTER 23

Mindfulness

O the mind, mind has mountains . . .

–Gerard Manley Hopkins

M ountains are ancient beings; they were here long before humans. To gaze at a large granite mountain is to be held in the cradle of Earth's history, reminded of a continuum of cascading effects that happen outside of immediate time and space.

With a full backpack on I can scarcely stand straight. I am climbing to base camp in preparation for summiting Mount Shasta in California. The backpack feels weighted down by rocks, and the trail is so steep in places I feel as if I will fall backward, ending up like an upturned beetle struggling to right myself. I am forced to climb slowly and carefully. I lean my weight fully on one leg while resting the other, in a manner of walking called the "rest step." This technique has long been used by mountain dwellers. I step, stop, match my breath to my stride, align with the rhythm of the mountain.

I had been invited to climb Shasta by a man I'd been dating for only a few months. His friends were reluctant to include me; they didn't trust me to stay the course and worried I'd prevent the group from reaching the summit.

One of the members kept rushing ahead, eager to prove he was capable of attaining Shasta's 14,179-foot peak, which we planned to tackle on the third day of our expedition. By day two he had hit the wall with dry heaves and headaches, the result of altitude sickness.

At high altitude, exposed to the elements, the simplest oversight— losing a glove or your footing, or rushing too fast—can have dire effects. The smallest thing can mean the difference between life and death. Mountains don't treat mistakes lightly.

As I snuggle into my tent before sleep, I think of what Aldo Leopold, one of the fathers of the modern ecological movement, learned from time spent in the mountains. Young and "full of trigger-itch," he and his friends come across a pack of wolves. Taught to believe that fewer wolves means more deer and better hunting, they shoot, killing an older wolf. Leopold approaches in time to see "a fierce green fire dying in her eyes." In that moment, he realizes that neither the wolf nor the mountain approve of what he's done.

From that point on, Leopold begins to "think like a mountain," mindful of the long-term consequences of his actions and the thread of connections that are not always visible to us in the moment. He comes to see that in time, killing wolves will cause the deer to proliferate and overgraze the mountain. The mountain will lose its vegetation, and the deer will starve.[1]

Mountains, ancient and abiding, offer a deep-time perspective. We normally think of mindfulness as relating only to the moment. But mountain consciousness reveals how each moment leads to other, hugely important moments. How a broken shoelace on the mountain can have cumulative and tragic consequences. Or how passing (or failing) an important exam, or offering a kind word, can have effects that ripple out way beyond the here and now. As you enter the mountains, you're invited to consider how each moment of mindfulness brings you into a vastness of time and space. The choices you make in the here and now will potentially have towering consequences in the future.

The Iroquois know this. Their council bases its decisions on the well-being of the Seventh Generation. The Iroquois aren't motivated solely by immediate needs, or self-willed desire. Their laws are de-signed to serve the whole tribe and the future of the tribe, 140 years out. They, too, are thinking like a mountain.

Today, we are destroying one of the oldest mountain ranges on the planet, the Appalachians. We're uprooting ancient forests, removing topsoil, and dynamiting as much as eight hundred feet of the mountaintops. All this destruction, simply to "efficiently" access more polluting coal to burn, is resulting in short-term monetary gain for a very few. These actions can never be undone. These mountaintops are gone forever, for the rest of human existence on Earth.

On Shasta, the slopes were at times so steep and icy that when passing by treacherous crevasses, we had to strap on crampons and rope together, each of us dependent on the others for our safety. That was how we reached the summit. Most of these people had been strangers to me just days before, but now we walked in rhythm, breathed as one body, joined and connected. *Rest, step, rest.*

Aren't we also roped together with all other beings through time and space and a series of connections we can barely decipher but nonetheless need to do our best to honor? We must step carefully, move slowly, progress mindfully.

The mountain permits nothing less.

Mindfulness Exploration

Make a practice of taking slow, meditative walks in a place you find beautiful, taking in everything about you. The walks can be as short as five minutes.

Some days, you might focus on touch, other days on scents or sight. Some days, you may simply choose to open your awareness as much as possible to your whole environment. Taking the same walk every day, attuning to changes and differences, can be a profound experience. As time goes by you will become increasingly aware not only of your surroundings but of how your presence impacts everything around you. Where you step, how heavily, even what you pay attention to, matters.

After each mindfulness walk, take a moment to reflect: "How do my everyday actions affect my safety and the well-being of all the Earth community, now and in the future?"

Capture whatever thoughts arise in your journal.

CHAPTER 24

Perspective

One climbs, one sees. One descends,
one sees no longer but one has seen.

–René Daumal

Climbing the mountain, we see things differently. The air becomes thinner; light, color, and sound have a greater clarity. What was once invisible becomes apparent.

What is it that you see now?

My first book, *Embrace Your Inner Wild,* came out in 2011, the result of a collaboration with wildlife photographer Don Moseman. I'd like to tell you his story.

From the age of nineteen until his mid-fifties, Don spent more than thirty years in San Quentin State Prison on San Francisco Bay, one of the toughest penitentiaries in the country and the only one in California with a Death Row. Spending hours of each day in his cell, Don gazed through the bars at Mount Tamalpais, the full-bodied mountain that dominates the local Marin County landscape. He decided that when he got out he would climb to the top. And in 1989, he did.

At the summit, Don reached out his arms. It was as if he held the entire bay within his two hands. The light bounced off the water, off the San Francisco skyscrapers, and flooded the distant horizon with a soft glow. Looking out, Don realized that he hadn't been anywhere or seen anything. He had spent most of his life incarcerated.

Mount Tamalpais stands only 2,574 feet high. As mountains go, it is quite small, but in Don's process of climbing to the top, everything changed. His view of the world—and his dream for his life—got bigger.

Don began walking to the 12-step meetings he attended to help him stay clean and sober. It didn't matter how far away the meeting, or how long the walk. San Francisco to San Mateo, a journey of twenty-five miles, was not unusual. But he didn't stop there. He kept walking, crossing America on foot, not once but three times, earning the nickname, Walkin' Don. He slept under the stars and in the rain, traipsed dusty trails, wore through multiple pairs of shoes, and lived large over thousands of miles. In committing to climbing one mountain, Don's view of his life expanded; it now stretched all the way to the far horizon.

More than any other landscape, the mountains shift our perspective. What we see and know at the bottom of the mountain is not what we see and know at the top. Here, above the tree line, the view broadens and widens; we are lifted out of the routine of our habitual life and granted a new vision.

Years after climbing Mount Ritter, the famous naturalist John Muir asked himself in his journal why the light seemed so much brighter on the top of the mountain after a difficult climb. His answer: ". . . the presence of danger summoned him to life."[1] Climbing Ritter infused Muir's life permanently with light—a knowing of what he had seen and overcome to stand at the peak. For Don and his ascent of Mount Tamalpais, the same held true.

In the steepest places, character is forged.

Climbing mountains, we prove to ourselves that we have the strength to do things. And in the process we are granted a new vision, one that would never have been available to us without the rigors of the climb, the height of the mountain, or the clarity of the air.

How we see things is how we make meaning of our lives. It shapes what we think, feel, and believe. At times, I have felt so stuck and blind about my next step that I have literally dashed up the hillside near my home just to see things differently. Sometimes we need the physical perspective of looking out from a great height in order to perceive our lives in a new light.

This is not the ego's journey—the desire to climb the ladder of success—but the journey of the soul. A true "peak" experience is remarkably devoid of self-centeredness. We climb the mountain not to conquer the world but to reach the higher ground—and thus the higher vision—within ourselves.

I've heard Don share his story many times. He is grateful for and incredulous of the life he has today. He likes to laugh that he has gone from prison inmate to published photographer—and that's quite a climb! A photographer, after all, is someone who applies his or her unique vision to seeing the world. And Don now has a wondrously large, wide-angled vision of life—one that he generously shares in order to inspire others, including those who still suffer behind bars.

In that cell, all those years back, Don could never have imagined what he has now: many years sober, hundreds of friends, skill with a camera, a profound connection to nature. When he stood at the top of Mount Tamalpais, he didn't imagine those precise things either, but of this I am sure: by taking a risk, by rising above his circumstances, by leaving his tiny cell and answering the call of the tallest mountain for miles around, he discovered his life could be different.

Sometimes we need the mountaintop perspective to see through the eyes of the soul.

Perspective Exploration

Allow yourself to enter fully into the perspective of a mountain that rises so tall and sees so far. To get in the spirit, you might want to climb a flight of stairs, or a big hill, or even a local mountain.

Then, simply stand, straight backed and strong, taking a few deep breaths as you feel into your mountain being. This is the part of you that carries the higher vision for your life.

When you sense your vision expanding, get out your journal and write about your life from the perspective of the mountaintop. What do you see from this "big picture" place? What is available to you here that isn't available to you when you're scurrying around in the every-dayness of life?

Start your reflection write with these words, "This is what I see . . ."

CHAPTER 25
Humility

. . . a peak can exercise the same irresistible
power of attraction as an abyss.

–Théophile Gautier

A time will come when you are called to the mountains in pursuit of your higher calling. You have a dream you want to realize, or a desire to come to know the great soaring spirit of your higher self. You want to touch the divine within. But the mountains confront you, daunting and towering. How will you climb them?

For John Muir, the mountains around Tuolumne Meadows in the Sierras signified a sacred place of soaring peaks that broke the harsh dividing line between Earth and Heaven. He wrote about the mountains often, and his ascent of Mount Ritter in particular.

As he ascended Ritter, Muir moved beyond the realm of the familiar: the landscape now barren of trees, the cheery notes of the sparrows a distant memory. Confronted by granite and silence, Muir experienced both deep awe and a tremendous sense of aloneness, as we perhaps all feel at the most significant moments of our lives.

As Muir progressed, he eventually confronted what appeared to be "an insurmountable rock face." Muir was paralyzed. Neither able to go forward nor climb back down, his "doom appeared fixed." Then he writes, "I seemed suddenly to become possessed of a new sense. The other self, bygone experiences, Instinct or Guardian Angel,—call it what you will,—came forward and assumed control. Had I been borne aloft upon wings, my deliverance could not have been more complete."[1]

John Muir's climb was grounded in his boundless love for the mountains—his deep reverence for the Sierras, and his humility in the face of them. What is the deep love and humility that will bring the gods to your side when you confront your insurmountable obstacle? What (or who) will help you overcome your fears and achieve the impossible?

When you stand in awe of others' feats, or wonder at times how you managed to complete a challenging project or learn a new skill or take a stand for something of value, you can know that you are carried by a more-than-human strength.

In the moment when Muir confronts almost certain death, whether he survives or not isn't the most critical thing. If he had died, he would have fallen to his death while following the path he loved most, on the mountain he loved most.

To follow a higher calling always involves a kind of death. You have to let go of what no longer serves your soul. Old beliefs will need to be sacrificed along the way. The journey is dangerous. You may fail, come to grief, lose everything. But you may also discover that when you walk the paths of the gods, you will find within yourself a grace and greatness that you never knew you had.

And you must hold that lightly too.

We were never meant to live at high altitude. The air is too thin. The people who find it hard to descend are those who mistake godly powers for their own, and they cling to the peak. They believe they arrived at the mountaintop on their own steam alone, and that they deserve to remain in these rarified heights. But the mountaintop can never be truly conquered. We can enter the realm of the gods, but we do not become them.

Mount Kailash in Tibet is considered so sacred that to set foot on her flanks is to defy the gods and risk death. To climb her would be sacrilege. It would steal from our souls. If we climb motivated only by ego, we lose part of our souls as well. And when we arrive at the summit, the power we wield is almost invariably toxic.

When we dedicate our climb to something bigger than our personal ambitions, we climb with humility. In this way, our journey becomes a sacred one—whether it be about building our careers, finding our true selves, or creating a better world for our grandchildren. When we attain the mountain peak, we rest there gratefully, conscious of all the help we have been given on our way to success.

If you climb with humility, the descent becomes easier as well.

When you descend the mountain with the love and attention you brought to ascending, you will learn to move freely within the vertical realm, navigating the highs and lows of life with equal nimbleness. Descending the mountain with care means taking the time to integrate what you learned on the peak, so you can bring that higher wisdom into your everyday life.

You may enter a brief depression, spiraling down into the dark canyons of your soul for a while. This is not unusual after experiencing a "high." It is simply part of the journey. Hold the depths lightly too, and you will come to see that all places are equally sacred.

You will come to see that, whether you are in the Heavens, Earth, or the Underworld, if you walk humbly and truly you will always bring the gods to your side.

Humility Exploration

Recall a time when you received guidance to overcome a difficult situation, either physical or emotional. What was the "new sense" that you became possessed of? What do you believe helped you through? Was it your higher self, your past experiences, your instincts, your "Guardian Angel," or something else entirely?

Allow yourself to feel, touch, taste, and fully embody the experience as you write about it in your journal.

If you have yet to have such an experience, simply recall a situation that is challenging you right now and spend some time writing about it in your journal. Imagine how you might be helped. What "new sense" would you like to be possessed of?

Next, whether you are writing about an actual event or an imagined one, reflect on these questions:

What was the nature of my mountain calling?

What was the obstacle that confronted me, both internally or literally?

Who or what were the allies on my journey?

What or who gives me strength?

What gives me humility?

After you've answered these questions in your journal, take a moment to reflect on the wisdom you have gained.

CHAPTER 26

Friction

Great things are done when men and mountains meet...

–William Blake

Earth is volatile. She slides, erupts, collides. Only by releasing formidable energy is the land shaped and formed into its dramatic contours. This energy can build up over hundreds of years or millennia. The longer the tension is held, the more power it has to shake and shift the landscape.

Africa glides into the southern tip of Europe, and the Alps rise up, at their center, three miles high. A 2005 earthquake in Pakistan causes the mighty Himalayas, home to the tallest mountain on Earth, to rise another five meters. Magma builds up over hot spots. The eruption of Krakatoa in 1883 hurls pumice thirty-four miles into the air that falls 3,313 miles away ten days later. The 2011 earthquake that strikes near the east coast of Japan shifts the main island by a staggering eight feet.

Earth's power isn't in her rigidity but in her ongoing dynamism; she is energetic, restless, creative, and destructive. When pressure accumulates, you know something new is trying to break through. Resistance is where energy resides.

We humans are also fiery and fusion filled, hot bellied like a furnace and boulder strong. And yet, for many of us, expressing anger—or any form of overt power—is frightening. We've been instructed to quell our fury and our passions. Alternatively, our heated emotions can be misdirected into physical aggression rather than spiritual power. When people and situations rub us the wrong way, sparks fly. Resistance causes friction. It ignites us. Something strikes our imaginations and we're on fire.

Linda, a workshop participant, put it this way: "The mountain's surface is beautiful, but my climb must be of the substance of the mountain. I must allow that magma to rise in me."

Owning our inner power is essential if we are to have an impact. Martin Luther King Jr. and Mahatma Gandhi understood how mountains are built: an irresistible force meets an immovable object. Their form of peaceful resistance collided with the outmoded and rigid thinking of their times, altering the topography of our world.

The fact that many of us are in opposition to the present worldview is both terrifying and electrifying. In every corner of the planet, people are creatively expressing new ways of being. We feel the restlessness and sense of disruption that precedes great change. Mountain wisdom tells us that nothing on Earth is solid; the future is always waiting to rise anew.

You can be moving along effortlessly in your life, but until you meet with resistance, you may have a difficult time discovering your inner strength. If you are perpetually conflict avoidant, if you want everything to be nice and everyone to love you, your inner power will probably elude you.

In 2010, I was set to self-publish a book of ecological and spiritual reflections and images with wildlife photographer Don Moseman. I had spent months selecting from thousands of his amazing pictures and pairing them with my reflections. I'd fallen in love with what we had created together. Then the blow came: Don confessed his hard drive had died, and none of the original photographs were recoverable.

I was beside myself. I believed in my bones that this book was part of my mission. I had worked so hard, done all the right things, or so I felt, and now this. In the midst of my despair, I had a dream:

I am standing on a high, narrow mountain path. Before me, a white-bearded, punishing god throws down boulders and blocks my way. I've been frightened of him all my life. But I'm too furious to care. I scream at him, "I don't give a damn, you're not stopping me." His eyes are wild and furious, but I am more furious. I will not be stopped.

I awoke peaceful and calm. I asked Don to go out and take more pictures. We were going to complete the book. All the photos in *Embrace Your Inner Wild* were taken in a one-year period. By the end of the year we didn't just have a beautiful book; we had a publisher. The book came out in November 2011.

My dream represented a profound shift for me. Unable to have children, I carried a deep belief that I wasn't worthy of giving birth. I wondered if I was being punished by an unforgiving god, and in some corner of my mind, I suspected that the book would miscarry too. But when the loss of the book seemed inevitable, something rose up in me. I was finally ready to face my shame and let go of any self-sabotaging thoughts that stood in my way.

Friction fuels our soul journey. It releases a prodigious amount of energy that creates the potential for new possibilities. Like the Earth, we rise and fall and renew ourselves. Only then do we take the first step onto terra nova—the new land of our life.

Friction Exploration

Find a place outside and plant your feet firmly on the ground, about hip width apart. Straighten your back and gently pull in your belly muscles. Stand tall like a mountain.

When you're ready, slowly lift your arms straight above your head and rub your palms together. Feel the heat generated by the friction. (If you can't stretch your arms above your head, simply rub your hands together in a way that's comfortable.)

When you notice a shift in your energy level and can feel the warmth generated by rubbing your hands together, begin a short journal entry with the words:

"I am the mountain who . . ."

Allow whatever wants to emerge to burst forth, unedited.

When you've finished writing, reflect back on what you have learned about your mountain self.

CHAPTER 27
Influence

I hope they never get a rope on you, weather . . .

–May Swenson

I stood on the summit of Mount Shasta as the storm hit. Clouds turned the purple of three-day-old bruises, and howling winds took up residence on the mountain and beneath my skin. Lightning struck. The first bolt hit so close I smelled burning, tasted iron on my tongue. My hair stood up like tree branches and my friends' faces glowed bone white in the electric air. We needed to get down the mountain—and fast. And yet, as the air spat fireworks, I lingered. I felt the pure energy of the sky and mountain pulsing through me; I was ecstatic, and terrified, and very much alive.

Mountains create their own weather. When air currents collide with rock, they're thrust upward, and as they rise, they cool. Clouds form, rain spills, snow falls. Steep-sloped mountains become flood chutes, spilling deluges into the valleys. On the leeward side of the mountain, away from the wind, lies the rain shadow: dry, dusty, desertlike.

Mountains shape the landscape, not just because they rise above it but because their stance is rock solid.

When we stand strong in our own beliefs, we also learn to dance with energy. Authenticity is power. Living in accordance with our own wild souls, we make our own weather. We hum with life. Like the wind, energy is only visible through its manifestation in the material world. It can arrive as a cleansing breeze or a wild keening. It can cut to the

109

quick or create an atmosphere of calm. In Hebrew, the word for wind, *ruach*, is also the word for god, breath, spirit. Energy has the power to uplift, inspire, and tear down. And yet, failing to connect to our deepest selves, we struggle to wield it wisely.

The hardest thing for some of us is to ground our lives in our values rather than our to-do lists. Busyness has become one of the commandments of modernity. Being constantly productive earns us the world's appreciation, even if our lives feel as if they're tumbling downslope. Making matters worse, our schools and workplaces seem to care only for those parts of us that an increasingly commercial society deems valuable. The totality of who we are—our essential self—is ignored in favor of extracting and then favoring only a tiny portion of our passion and purpose. Fragmented, fractured, we strive harder, do more, and yet frequently fail to rise to become the bigger and more bountiful versions of ourselves. And our ability to deeply influence the world in a positive way becomes ever more elusive.

But what if true power were less about doing and more about knowing who we are?

Mountains reveal the strength that comes with integrity—wholeness, entirety. The base of the mountain and its peak are both part of one integral system. Just as every part of us—body, mind, and spirit—is integral to who we are. Living in integrity, we live according to a strong set of values, every aspect of us an expression of our essential nature. Commented one of my workshop participants, "So often soaring and rooting seem to be at odds, yet the mountain holds both truths."

For centuries, the mystics who made their home in the mountains cared nothing for the prosaic activities of civilization. Inhabiting the spine of the Earth, they lived close to the essence of who they were in prayer and contemplation. This is the way of mountains, power that is intrinsic—influence that comes from deep within the soul. If we are to responsibly embody our own dynamic power, we need to explore the mountain of the undiscovered self. We need to know ourselves deep in the bone.

On the top of Mount Shasta, as I experienced intense waves of energy passing within and around me, I felt a pure energy that spoke its own language, resonant and real and rooted to the core of the mountain. When the same primal energies swirl about us, when we are blasted by ferocious winds and towering tempests, we, too, can learn to stand our ground. In remaining strong in ourselves, we discover our innate power to alter and redirect energy, and by so doing, we change the rest of the world.

For in the end, the weather we create in turn carves us, shapes us over time to reveal the essence of who we are. In the words of the eighth-century poet Li Po,

We sit together, the mountain and me,
until only the mountain remains.[1]

Influence Exploration

Notice your shadow at different times of day . . . behind you, in front of you. Walk, and watch how your shadow passes over everything around you . . . a flower is shaded, a paving stone turns dark gray, the ground is cooler for your passing.

And it is not just the ground that is touched. Everything between your body and the body of Earth is influenced by your presence: the air, insects, pollen, water molecules.

We are constantly influencing everything around us, all the time, whether we are aware of it or not.

As you continue to walk, gently reflect on these questions:

What kind of influence would I like to have?

What would it look like?

What values would it be based on?

Who or what would it affect?

Explore your responses in your journal.

∾ Leaving the Mountains ∾

After time spent in the mountains, do you feel stronger in yourself, more aware of your ability to impact the world?

What most challenges you?

What most excites you?

If you were to fully embody your mountain being, who would you have to become? What would allow you to step into the highest vision for yourself and your life?

No one is meant to live long on the mountaintop, but the wisdom we find in the mountains can affect profound changes both in our personal lives and in the larger world.

Take your time descending from the mountains as you reflect on the essence of what you want to integrate and apply to your life right now.

PART 5
Grasslands

*I will speak to you in the language of grasslands,
answer with your own greening song.*

The Cosmic Spirit seeks not to restrain us
But lifts us stage by stage to wider spaces.

–Hermann Hesse

The steppes of Asia, the pampas of South America, the tundra of northern Europe, the prairies and plains of the North American heartland, the rangelands of Australia, and the great African savannahs from which all of humanity arose. Home to the great migratory mammals and the first hunter-gatherers, grasslands sweep across the planet, covering a quarter of Earth's surface.

Grasslands are fields of possibility, frontiers of hope. They live large in our imaginations and our literature: Walt Whitman's *Leaves of Grass*, Willa Cather's *My Antonia*, Laura Ingalls Wilder's *Little House on the Prairie*, the great dust bowl of John Steinbeck's *The Grapes of Wrath*, the stories of pioneers headed west across an inland ocean of grass.

Hardship is seeded into the history of the grasslands, but also community, rich land, and rolling hills that welcome us. In sun-buttered meadows and lush valleys, far away from dark mountains and brooding forests, we build our settlements, make our homes, and learn to cultivate both the land and what we value.

On the mythical level, the grasslands also represent the place of the hero's return. In the grasslands we return to community to seed and share our newfound wisdom for the greater good. And yet, as with any hero's journey, the return comes with challenges. How do we integrate the knowledge we've gained? How do we settle into everyday life after our grand adventures? How will our gifts be received?

Like the prairies that balance open space and expansive freedoms with the deep rootedness of the grasses—literally hundreds of plant species woven into an interdependent whole—the grasslands challenge us to find balance between living as authentic, unique beings and as part of a community.

Do you long to put up a picket fence and create a small and cozy place to call home, with a patch of land to plant and tend? Or, like the great hunter-gatherers and other migratory beings, do you yearn to be free to roam the boundless terrain? The grasslands celebrate both ways of being, as long as we live in a way that serves the whole community.

If you find yourself struggling with the grasslands soulscape, you may be one who is challenged by the simple and steady dedication of making a life. How often do you start something but don't stay with it? Have you tilled your soil sufficiently? Do you run out of patience before what you sow can be harvested? We don't have to belong to a geographic place, but we have to commit to something in our lives—something more than just ourselves—in order to become whole, in order to contribute our unique gifts to the world.

Exploring the grasslands, we discover ways in which to nurture our own particular blossoming and that of our communities. How do we grow our gratitude? Bring more light into our spirits? Learn how to flourish with the ease and naturalness of prairie wildflowers?

When we make our home in the grasslands, we are at peace with who we are and what we have to offer to life. We take our gifts and plant them in rich soil, where their seeds can blossom and we can bloom—for the greater good of all.

CHAPTER 28
Belonging

*Give up all other worlds
except the one to which you belong.*

–David Whyte

Every day the prairie dogs emerge from their dens before dawn. They press their hands together as if in prayer, and stand and watch the sunrise for twenty or thirty minutes at a time. In the evening, they turn toward the setting sun and again press their paws together, as in utter stillness they watch the light fade and night descend.

Author Terry Tempest Williams spent a summer observing the rituals of a small community of Utah prairie dogs, creatures of the grasslands. As she grew to understand them, they appeared to her to hold a reverence for their place in the world that we, in our fractured lives, have lost. Williams asks, "What do they know that we have forgotten?"[1]

I take a trail several times a week that travels through open grassland. The other day, something caught my attention. Several hundred yards away—a dark shape. Perhaps a rock, I thought. But how would it have gotten there, into the middle of the field? The grass around the shape was green, threaded with the remains of summer's gold. I recognized the fine crisscross lines made by the coyote and other mammals that roam these lands. The brown rocklike shape sat like a punctuation mark at end of one of these paths. Maybe a deer? I moved toward it slowly, willing my feet soundless on the damp ground.

When I was about sixty feet away, the brown rock rose like baked bread. Then a pair of ears emerged, followed by two alert eyes, and a healthy young bobcat stood before me.

The more I come to know and love the box canyon of Pacheco Valle* where I live, the more is revealed to me. Pileated woodpeckers, loping coyotes, singing grasses, mad swarms of early-spring swallows are gifts of this intimacy. The way we come to know and care for a lover's skin— every scar, curve, and slope more familiar to us with touch and time.

My friend, a landscape architect, tells me that a place feels beautiful to us when we feel integral to it—a part of it in some way. What is it that draws your soul inexplicably and powerfully to certain regions? What places do you belong to? What places molded you? William Faulkner declared that however much he wrote he could never fully exhaust his "little postage stamp of native soil."[2] There is a "native soil" in all of us—that place that most shapes our thoughts, experiences, and ways of interacting with the world.

The roots of the grasslands grow deep and wide, weaving an immense, fibrous tapestry under the earth. When we look out at a sea of grass, we see only the tip of the life force: most of the biomass of the prairie is found underground. And it is this deep attachment to the soil that makes the prairies strong and viable. The grasslands teach us that being rooted is vital. Anything that is not firmly planted in the earth—a stray object, a shallow-rooted tree—gusts away.

When the John Deere plough came to the prairies and began to till the soil, it cut deep, uprooting gnarly roots from the rich ground. Some protested that this was madness, declaring that we would lose the soil if we tore up the roots. Within a couple of decades they were proved right. Mountain-high dust storms blasted the southern plains; one, in April of 1935, even reached across Nebraska, the Midwest, and on toward Washington, DC. The soil of the prairie, loosed from its attachment to the grass roots, began a great migration of its own. And the Okies, as the prairie farmers became known, soon followed.

---

* Valle is spelled without a "Y"

And hasn't the modern world made loess (windblown soil) of us all? Haven't we, too, been uprooted, the tapestry of connection lost to the whirl of our modern, mobile, urban society? Strip malls don't just steal the identity of a place, but treat us as if we are also lifeless and don't matter; they want nothing from us other than our money. When we destroy the character of a place and replace it with the convenience of sameness and anonymity, we become lonelier, less connected, less part of the fabric of life.

The Lakota people, the great tribespeople of the prairies had a term: "Mitakuye Oyasin." Translated, these words mean "all my relations." When we live in a place that we know and love, every being supports and nurtures us. We are never alone.

This is the grasslands as poetry: interconnected, interrelated, drawn close together. It is a circle of women meeting to sew, of neighbors gathering to help raise a new home. It is borrowing tools and sharing food. It is working the land together and celebrating as family. It is the prairie dogs, living within the earth and close to each other in highly social communities. It is bringing our hands together to give thanks for the native soil—the patch of Earth—to which each of us belongs.

Belonging Exploration

Early in the morning and in late evening, take a few minutes to stand still, breathe deeply, and, like the prairie dogs, place your hands together and practice giving thanks for your place in the world. If you live somewhere that doesn't feel like home, this exploration will likely challenge you. Yet acknowledging your gratitude for the sun, the air, the soil beneath the pavement, the patch of light on a lawn, the beauty of a sunset, can help transform your relationship to your local environment, whether it be a dense urban setting or a more natural one.

As a nightly practice, write a gratitude list of all the things your home ground gifted you with that day, however small or seemingly insignificant. As you become accustomed to being grateful, notice: do you feel a greater sense of belonging within yourself? If so, how do you experience this feeling?

Chapter 29
Sensuality

and your very flesh shall be a great poem . . .

–Walt Whitman

I must have been five years old, not much older. The grasses grew taller than my head, and all above me the thick blue sky stretched out like a tent. I watched a round bee wriggle into the pollen of sunflowers as if taking a bath. Far away my mother's voice called me in to dinner, while I dissolved into the sticky, insect-buzzing warmth of a late summer day in an English meadow.

Looking back, I believe that the soft grass of England was my first lover, teaching me that my body responds to a soft, slow touch, to vibrations of sound, to whispers on my skin—the tickling touch of stalks.

Yet how many of us place our bodies next to the Earth's anymore?

Sensuality is seeded in intimacy and thrives on proximity. We burrow into our mother's wombs, and later, wriggle and crawl over the ground, touching and tasting and smelling everything. To be in touch with our sensuality is to naturally bloom, to connect with the very spirit of creation. Life arises through contact; it thrives on familiarity and closeness, as do we.

Far away from the dense forest and the towering mountain, a meadow is the perfect, light-filled playground to explore the relationship between our bodies and the body of the Earth. Here, we rest in the lap of the world, hidden and protected by long grasses and serenaded by fluting birdsong. Meadows hold us and enfold us in the sweet-smelling breath of the planet.

Right now, bushes and flowers and soft grasses are everywhere around me. Hummingbirds, more than I have ever seen in one place, swoop and flash in brilliant colors, and fragrant pine scent wafts through the open window. I am at a writer's refuge in Point Reyes, Northern California. In every way it is the perfect spot to ponder the beauty and lushness of the meadows.

I take my journal outside to sit among the grasses and flowers, turning my face toward the mid-October sun. I think about the Earth waiting patiently, for a billion years, for the sun's heat to penetrate her barren bones until, finally, she awakened to life. Later, from her soft flesh erupted the first greenery, the first colorful flowers, and, in time the pollinators that would spread those lush blooms across her entire body.

And don't you also flourish with the sun's attention, with a soft, warm touch?

For too long we've neglected the wisdom and needs of our bodies. Cementing over the planet, we've separated not only from her body, but our own earthly bodies as well. We have lost the innate sense of what it is to rise headlong in spring to the touch of the sun, to be lush and green in our beings.

The manicured lawn, which first emerged in seventeenth-century England, was an attempt to bring the beauty of open meadows or forest glades into our everyday lives. In North America, lawns came to unite the fronts of houses with a democratic, free-flowing river of green.

But the lawn, though intended for tranquil pleasures, in reality demands constant watering, fertilizing, dosing of chemicals—and cutting! Rather than relaxation, it promotes a Puritan ethic of good order and hard work. It tames what is wild. It screams control.

Meadows are different. They bloom naturally. They come to fruition in their own time, according to their own rhythm.

Overwork and stress are the enemies of sensuality. The word "stress" comes from the French word *estresse*, which means narrowness and oppression. Frantically busy, falling always further behind, we shut ourselves off from the beauty of the moment and our own animal nature, which delights in the tactile, sensate pleasures of the world.

A meadow, in contrast, is an open palm, a body unfurled.

Last night as I walked back from my writing cabin through the garden to the main house for dinner, two small fawns were eating apples from a tree. The light was soft, and the bushes glowed. Hummingbirds whirred by like madcap angels among the flowers, gathering every last bit of the day's sweetness. The clouds, shredding against the setting sun, cast soft lavender shadows over the marshes.

I stood and watched as the smallest fawn moved through the grasses toward me on knock-kneed, spindly legs, his large, shiny black nose twitching. His ears, like satellite dishes, opened toward me; his curiosity, like my own, drawing us together; his soft mouth on the yellow apple, so close I could almost taste the apple's tartness on my tongue. All things gathered in this simple meeting, each of us satisfying our need for contact in the way we know best—by nuzzling up to the body of the Earth.

Sensuality Exploration

Visit a park, meadow, or any fieldlike setting. Pack a picnic basket of delicious foods and a favorite beverage. Wear your most comfortable and colorful clothes. This day is to be dedicated to sensuous exploration. Touch Earth: walk barefoot, run your fingers over the petals of flowers, feel the kiss of the wind and the sun. Allow your whole body to soak in the pure pleasure of connecting to nature.

As you savor the day, take a moment to reflect in your journal:

What have I learned about my own sensual nature?
How can I bring more sensuality into my life?
What might change if I did?

CHAPTER 30
Resilience

This new green of spring lives everywhere in me.

–Cyncie Winters, workshop participant

The day comes when something rises in you out of winter's earth. Grass, stalk, leaf unfurl beneath a lemon sun. The juice and joy of the world revisit you. Imagination stirs; a poem arises. The great greening of the soul begins.

Youthful, playful, pushy, green has no patience with restraint. It bursts on the scene and spreads over the land, freely and fully. It is the way you feel when you're in love. It springs in you, beats in your blood, streams through your veins. It is experienced in sap, and sass, and gusto. You could no more stop it than a field can resist the greening of spring.

Green is the dominant color of flora and fauna and all that is most resilient in you. It is the ever-flowing expression of imagination. It is the creative energy released at the beginning of the Universe that streams through the sun to Earth to be captured by plants. It is the food we eat, the fuel that fires us, the spark that drives us.

It is the old woman I met at a writing conference who told me she'd been cut down and cut off, but nothing had killed her yet, and her poems kept flowing. It is the hope that saw me through the darkest year of my life, when I lost a baby to an ectopic pregnancy and my father to emphysema, and despair grew in me. It is my soul, black as earth, pushing its way through the darkness back to the light, back to lushness and the laughter. It is the rising of spirit after a long depression. It is the passion for life we carry like seeds in our heart.

It is the simple joy of being alive. And our souls drink it in.

Resilience Exploration

Recall a time when you felt exuberant, filled with creativity and an irrepressible passion for life. This is a discrete moment from your past, like a snapshot in an album only with all the details of texture, fragrance, and feeling. Write about the experience in the first person, present tense, recording all the sensations you can muster.

When you've written your piece, reflect on these questions:

What is the overall mood?
Who or what is present?
Where am I?

As you consider your answers, write a short reflection piece on what conditions are present when the greening of your soul takes place.

CHAPTER 31

Freedom

Whatever else prairie is—grass, sky, wind—it is most of all a paradigm of infinity. . .

–William Least Heat-Moon

The prairies once covered 40 percent of North America, extending from the tall blue grasses of the east to the Great Plains. So vast were they that you could travel for days and, seeing the unchanging landscape before you, feel as if you'd never moved from your starting place. Stretching for thousands of miles in shades of blue, purple, green, and gold that changed with the seasons and the spread of forbs and grasses, this was space that seemed to expand into infinity.

The prairie was the wide open field in which anything could happen. And in which we believed we could become anything we wanted.

Dusk cast purple shadows onto the land and the breeze rustled the tall grasses in the pampas of Chile. It was my twenty-second sobriety birthday. My feet, bootless, were resting after our fourteen-mile trek as I sat on a bench outside the *refugio* where we would stay the night. At dawn the next morning, my husband and I planned to hike up to the Torres, a high-mountain cirque. As I sat peacefully, I thought about the miles of pampas we'd covered, that day and in the many days beforehand. The wind was so strong at times it tossed me like tumbleweed. The sky, the grasses, the immense distances—exhilarating. The rushing air whipping up a sense of recklessness, a kind of crazy, blown-apart feeling that had me yelling back at the pummeling, ear-pounding wind. That wind, I heard told, drives many insane.

The prairies threatened even Walt Whitman. Such vastness sits easier in the imagination than when experienced firsthand. His great work *Leaves of Grass* was a metaphor for American democracy, yet on seeing the grasslands, he immediately referred to the "tree problem," by which he meant their absence, and proposed some be planted right away. Perhaps Whitman feared that without trees as landmarks to measure ourselves against, without something to give the eye and mind perspective, we were in danger of losing our sense of proportion and kinship.

But the true story of the prairies cannot be understood in what lies above the ground. It is written invisibly, but confidently, under the surface of the land.

For all their wild vastness, the grasslands are predicated on a deep inner restraint. The richness of the land comes from within and is constantly nourished and replenished by every member of the community. Grasshoppers drop a small portion of every leaf they clip to fall back into the earth. Dead roots are broken down and gradually built up into humus. When the sun delivers surplus energy, the plant community uses it to create and store nutrients that build soil, which in turn enhances the whole system. Even the lowliest dung beetle plays his part, turning the detritus of the other denizens into even richer soil.

Over the years the grasslands and her natural inhabitants have built up a capital of soil that benefits the whole system. The reason the prairies are so abundantly napped with clovers, lavenders, asters, gentians, and grasses is that they've learned to thrive within the set limits of a semiarid environment.

The grasslands teach us that true freedom isn't grounded in ego-based grandiosity or a rugged sense of individualism—with which it is often confused—but rather the simple dedication to a way of living that consistently cultivates our inner depths. Willing to live close to Earth, with a certain humility and awareness of our interlocking obligations and connections, we find the strength to live fully and freely as ourselves. If we want to experience real freedom, we need to continually build up the soil of our souls.

From the bench that evening, I watched the moon rise over the horizon and ignite the tips of the grasses. Though too far away to see, I imagined the guanaco, a delicate and lovely llamalike creature, playing in the silver light. I offered up a prayer of gratitude for my sobriety, acknowledging the stretch of years that lay behind me just as the day's trail now did. I had walked many, many miles from where I started.

In the silence of that night, the wind now astonishingly absent, I recollected that I drank to be free. I wanted a life without rules or responsibilities. I lived carelessly, even dangerously. I remembered one hot summer night on the island of Malta, drunk and in love. My boyfriend, Peter Paul, decided to drive at full speed along the winding coastline with only his feet on the driving wheel. Oblivious to the threat to others or ourselves and thrilled by our own daring, we sped heedlessly through the night.

In our various ways, each of us is seeking—whether consciously or not—to connect with our own sense of limitlessness: our divine nature. But we should not mistake this for a belief that we can have—or do—everything we want, whenever we want.

If our sacred quest to be at liberty to fulfill our own particular human potential becomes confused with material desire or self-centeredness, we lose touch with what it is to be truly free.

Over time I, too, had to learn the daily practice of giving back—of living not just for my own self-referential needs. I hadn't realized this was the way of true freedom.

All that I held in my heart that evening—my husband, work, writing, friendships—didn't come to me in an instant. They took time. My inner strength and knowing built up through the years of my sobriety. I learned to take responsible risks in my work and relationships. Ideas sprouted and bloomed. This was freedom without recklessness, and things grew from it. Like that perfect evening—the world at my feet as moonlight poured down and the sky stretched out forever.

The next day at dawn, my husband and I began the strenuous trek that would lead away from the pampas to the higher ground of the Andes. As the sky turned from pink to blue, I watched an Andean condor circling above, his ten-foot wingspan the widest of any living bird. He rode the thermals, the strength of his wings proclaiming his mastery of the open space in which he makes his home. And yet his eyes, too, remained focused on the ground.

Freedom Exploration

Take a walk outside with the express intention of paying attention to all the plants growing around you, trees to tulips. When you feel ready, turn your focus toward one particular plant. Notice how she blooms just as she should, but within limits.

After all, if the plant you are focused on were ten times larger, wouldn't she overshadow everything else? Mightn't she struggle to get enough water? Would she leave enough nutrients for the other plants in the neighborhood?

Spend some time contemplating that she might be the perfect size for her species and where she is growing.

Now take your focus into yourself. How can you fully and freely bloom within the limits imposed on you by your responsibility to others, human and nonhuman, and by Earth's finite resources?

Explore your responses in your journal.

CHAPTER 32

Beauty

To experience beauty is to have your life enlarged.

–John O'Donohue

The sight of spring wildflowers, an exquisite painting, or a sublime sunset can literally take our breath away. More often focused on the mundane, in these moments we stop and look around as if suddenly awake. Attention to the beautiful stirs our passions, puts us in touch with the wonder of life. We can leave an art gallery or a verdant meadow humming with excitement, longing to break free from all that holds us painfully closed.

Beauty can help us find the strength to take the next step or take a stand. Beauty entices us to fall in love, write poetry, sing out loud, create art, dance into the night, or sacrifice for something greater than ourselves. The sight of a beloved's face or a golden valley at dawn can inspire us to make significant changes in our lives.

The power of beauty is that it awakens our imaginations.

Naturally drawn to what we find lovely, we become like the honeybee that presses himself into the heart of the flower and then flies off to pollinate more loveliness in the world. Beauty binds everything together, drawing us into a circle of relationships. Beauty can be considered another name for love.

Yet when we talk of beauty we are often dismissed as idealistic or foolishly romantic. Bottom-line thinking cares nothing for beauty. Concerned with profits and growth, it favors malls over meadows, missiles over museums, and fossil fuels over fresh air. This "clear" thinking is the cause of so much pollution—both internal and external—we are sometimes literally blinded to our surroundings. Its black-and-white calculus represses the spontaneous flow of beauty, which, like a wildflower emerging through cement, wants to break free of confines and cages.

But what if we rebelled? What if we subjected every action, every notion, to the question posed by theologian Carolyn Gifford: "Is what we are doing, is what I am doing, beautiful or not?"[1]

It was 1998 and I had taken the threadbare trail up the hill above the Croatian city of Dubrovnik at first light. The Serbo-Croation war had ended three years before. The cable car that had once carried tourists up the steep hillside was a victim of the shellings, and I found myself entirely alone.

Below, the medieval city showed off its recently replaced red tile roofs; the Adriatic gleamed like sapphires. At the summit, the bare mountains of Bosnia faded away to the east like so many sharp teeth. But what took me entirely by surprise was the bright field of poppies that greeted me—rich, red, radiant.

I thought about the flowers that must have strewn the coffins of those who had died in the war. And saw the meadow, ablaze in the light of morning, as more enduring than the scars of battle, the beauty more real than the ugliness of hate, the flowers truer than the bullet holes that pockmarked the outside walls of the hotel where my husband and I were staying on our honeymoon.

Captivated by beauty, in that moment I could see beyond the brokenness of the world into something more enduring, more resilient, infinitely more lovely. Beauty, I thought, can break through anywhere, at any time, surprising us.

Writes the poet and farmer Wendell Berry, "Under the pavement, the dirt is dreaming of grass."[2] And what loveliness do you dream about? Like the poppies and the poets, do you long to draw attention to the world's beauty? Or like the bees, have you learned how powerful it is to celebrate beauty? That by dancing your appreciation for the wonders of this world, you can become a true leader, inspiring others to follow you? This is how beauty has the power to enchant us and change us.

When a bee colony outgrows its hive, scout bees are sent out to find a new location. They return to the colony to perform a waggle dance to communicate how enthusiastic they are about the potential of a new site.

Moving onto the *Apis* dance floor, they shake their behinds from side to side, run up and down creating a figure eight, then shake their behinds again vigorously and repeat the same moves. They dance for minutes, even hours, emitting a buzz and surrounded by curious on-lookers.

The more fervently they believe theirs is the perfect site, the longer they perform the dance. If other bees are dancing to promote different sites, all well and good. No time or energy is spent negating others' choices. They dance only to inspire, to enchant. If they dance long enough and enthusiastically enough, their site will incite the most curiosity and more and more bees will fly off to check it out. When enough bees approve it, the swarm is on.

One bee, expressing her appreciation through dance, can decide the fate of an entire colony.

What difference could you make if you decided to focus your energy on beauty?

Beauty Exploration

The African praise poem is part of a long and venerable oral tradition, and a way of honoring the praiseworthy essence at the heart of every living being. For your praise poem, choose something in nature you find beautiful: a flower, a tree, a particular season.

Begin your poem with

"Praise to . . ."

Then the second line with the words

"I am . . ."

Now continue to describe your subject in bold and tender terms.

For example . . .

Praise to the wild iris
I am brightness, robed in splendor.
When bees see me they dip their heads in pleasure.
When I vanish from the fields, you will still look for me,
Even though you know I am gone.

As I wrote this poem, I realized that I always look for wild irises long after they have withered and died. Their beauty is etched inside me. But I also recognized something else: I feel the same way about my creativity as I do about irises. Whenever I lose sight of it, I'm always anticipating its return.

Now it is your turn to write some praise poems. Head outside and have fun. This is not about writing great poetry but about praising the beauty of this world.

When you've written your praise poem, reflect on what it has taught you about the importance of beauty.

Explore your discoveries in your journal.

CHAPTER 33

Openness

We are fields before each other.

–Thomas Aquinas

"Something there is that doesn't love a wall," writes the poet Robert Frost.[1] The meadow is an open space without walls or fences. Here is life on a human scale, miles apart from the lofty schemes of economics and world events that dominate our existences. In the meadows, we stand on common ground, in a place of togetherness, where the common good outranks the rights of a few. In this state of communion we come to see that we touch each other, need each other, are part of each other.

Once, after making love during those first sheet-tousled weeks of getting to know each other, my husband said, "My heart is open to you." I rested my head on his chest and heard the drumbeat of his heart. I relaxed, knowing now that Bruce would wait for me to step in and share his space when I was ready. No guards, no fences, no defenses: this tall, kind man was spreading his love out like an open meadow, inviting me in, in my own time.

We experience the sacred not in isolation but in connection to an idea, a person, a place, or another living being. In community, we thrive and flourish. We may idolize the rugged loner, particularly in American culture, but our souls crave connection.

Writes anthropologist Margaret Mead, "Nobody has ever before asked the nuclear family to live all by itself in a box the way we do. With no relatives, no support, we've been put in an impossible situation."[2] We are more content and secure working together.

And yet we remain a culture of wall makers. We divide mind from body, human from non-human, soul from soil. In settling the prairies, the pioneers used so much barbed wire, also known as devil's rope, that it could have wrapped around the globe twenty-five times. The devil's rope provided boundaries for the settlers and gave them ownership of the land. It also did more to destroy the prairies than even the John Deere plough. Fenced in, the bison and other migratory animals could no longer move at will in search of food, and so they starved. These grassland grazers, so essential to the prairie's ecosystem, couldn't survive within the newly circumscribed land.

In personal terms, we talk about the need for boundaries, to have our own space. Today each member of a household may well have his or her own personal entertainment system. No need to even gather around the communal TV set anymore, as we once gathered around the campfire.

Any system, including a meadow, is part of a whole. But we humans have tended to focus on ourselves as if our species were a separate entity rather than integral to something larger and altogether more interrelated. We forget that we are porous beings. The world doesn't stop at the border of our skins; we are part of the matrix of life.

I drive out to Point Reyes National Seashore and sit on a fallen log in a large meadow. The sky is hung with dark hammock clouds, the air swimming with the salty fragrance of ocean. A riot of pink lilies sings out from the golden grasses. A fir tree grows beside me, extravagant in its gestures with so much space to fill. This is one of my favorite places in the world. I feel completely at home here and never lonely. So it is the perfect spot to contemplate the fears that can cause me to shut down emotionally or set myself apart.

I take a deep breath, aware that in this wide-open meadow I have no defenses. A mountain lion could spy me from far off. Rain could drench me in an instant. Open spaces make us vulnerable. The open spaces *inside* us as well. An open society is a vulnerable society; those who would destroy it have easy access. But a closed society is a suffocating one. It destroys itself from within.

Staying open is challenging. It takes courage to fling open the doors of your heart and welcome whatever comes. No objects, only subjects. No "it," only "thou." Every visitor made welcome.

Writes Rilke:

Let no place in me hold itself closed,
for where I am closed, I am false . . .[3]

What will it take to open our hearts to each other and our planet? To become large and free enough within ourselves to realize that we are on this amazing Earth journey together? What common purpose, if not our planetary crisis that touches each and every living thing, will draw us together?

One night while driving home, I encountered a herd of deer grazing in the meadow that sits at the opening of my valley, their antlers a forest of silver branches under a full moon. I stopped the car and slowly got out, taking a few quiet steps into the grasses. A large buck raised his head, otherwise indifferent to my presence. A few other eyes turned in my direction, then down again, their grazing resuming. Scientists tell us that everything we see, hear, touch is governed not by immutable laws but by relationship. Touch. Contact. Connection. Hardly daring to breathe, I sat down, claiming my space in the commons. For this one moment, included in the herd.

Openness Exploration

Think of a person, situation, idea, or new direction in life you want to open up to. Then find a place in your environment that appears to embody a quality of openness.

Settle in, breathing gently and comfortably. Relax your muscles, open up your heart center, and allow your focus to soften, so that the edges between things blur and meld.

When you are ready, introduce the person, situation, part of yourself, belief, or direction that you want to learn to embrace. Breathe out any tension. Simply allow this being or feeling to share your space for the moment.

Continue to hold this open space until you feel a sense of acceptance, or any other feeling that wants or needs to emerge.

Then spend some moments reflecting on your experience in your journal.

Do you feel you have opened up?

How does this openness serve you, your life?

Do you feel closer to yourself and others?

What are the next steps you need to take to remain more open?

∽ Leaving the Grasslands ∽

The grasslands invite us to explore our relationship to place, self, community. Here, in the open plains and playful meadows, we examine the richness of small moments and the depths of our ties to Earth and each other.

As you leave the grasslands, what insights will you take away?

What other thoughts or images do you want to keep exploring?

Are there any seeds that need planting right now?

As you look back at this fertile and flower-filled landscape, consider for a moment what you want to plant for the good of your family, work, life, community.

How will you be a part of the great flourishing of our precious planet?

Walking the Wild Edge

You walking, your footprints are
the road, and nothing else

–Antonio Machado

I have come to Point Reyes Seashore to ponder the ending of this book. The wetlands where I sit is an ecotone, a tidal zone, where the waters from the Pacific pour in to meet the land. When two bioregions converge, as here, we find the greatest proliferation of life: the most species and entirely unique plant and animal forms.

We, too, are ecotone beings: edge-walkers—navigating the fine line between wildness and modernity. Both forces meet in us, twenty-first-century citizens who use computers and drive cars but who are also creatures of the Earth.

How do we hold this balance?

In this mix of high-tech modernity and wildness is a profound and curious power that we have barely begun to explore or understand. We cannot return to a completely indigenous way of life, nor would we want to. We must learn to navigate this place where the old ways and the new coincide. An ecotone is a transition zone—a crucible for change that poses both great peril and extraordinary opportunity. We don't know how it will play out.

What is important is that we take small steps to redress the imbalance that leans evermore toward the linear and mechanistic. Plant a garden, send your kids outside to play, share your stories about birds, or creeks, or the gentle sway of a beloved tree. Celebrate the way the sun pours through the windowpane, casting prisms of light.

A friend who was never particularly drawn to the outdoors began to walk for thirty minutes every morning in a small wilderness area. When the Parks and Recreation Department announced plans to build a kids' playground under the tall cottonwoods, home of nesting fowl, she joined with three hundred others to stop it from happening. Falling in love with wildness, she became fierce in her protection of it, like the mother goshawk that dive-bombed my husband, talons bared, to safeguard her nest.

I imagine when my friend and her community refused to allow the ground to be invaded for digging boxes and climbing towers across the trail from the dens of the red fox, Earth and all her inhabitants cheered her on.

We must draw from the natural world to feed our souls, and then give back in return. We are in a reciprocal dance with the Earth. We breathe the same wild air, thrive on the same waters, are infused with the same sunlight. If we don't reclaim and come to love our inner wildness, how much more of the Earth's wild places will we be willing to destroy?

Our work is just beginning.

In having the courage and willingness to explore the wild realm of your own soul, you have already accessed significant strength and wisdom to live your life more fully, giving of your own particular gifts. As you continue to integrate the many aspects of your wild soul that you encountered on this journey, you will only become more alive to yourself and the possibilities for your life and work.

For now, take a moment to reflect on where you've been and what you've experienced. Did certain landscapes call to you? Did you struggle with others that hold your shadow and your growing edge? Did your relationship to certain landscapes change and evolve? How does your journey through the landscapes inform you about your life today?

Wherever you find yourself, know that it is the perfect place to be. Evolution doesn't unfold in straight and predictable lines. It spins and swirls, meets dead ends, often needing to turn back on itself to find another, more fruitful path. And so will you. Give yourself over to the truth of this dynamic and surprising dance. Dedicate yourself to loving wildness as it lives in and around you—and you will be amazed.

If you continue on this path, you will experience evolutionary leaps and insights beyond your wildest imaginings. Spend time out of doors, praise the Earth, love the wild migrations of your own imagination, and be grateful for every leaf you meet. In this way, you will inevitably become part of the great rewilding of our world.

Let the following touchstones guide you and support you as you learn to walk in the mystery, grace, and beauty of wildness.

The Ten Touchstones of the Wild Soul

1. I feel my own flesh and the flesh of the Earth as one. In harming the Earth, I cause myself harm; in caring for the Earth, I care for myself.
2. I honor the Earth as a primary source of spiritual revelation.
3. I treat the Earth and all her inhabitants as relations to be honored and celebrated.
4. I open myself to the wild and creative energy of the Earth that seeks unique expression through me.
5. I respect the Earth's finite physical constraints while embracing the boundlessness of my spiritual nature.
6. I take regular breaks from technology and the human-built world in order to reconnect with nature and my own wild soul.
7. I bring a listening spirit to the Earth, recognizing that all beings are sacred and hold essential wisdom.
8. I protect, celebrate, and seek intimacy with the place on Earth in which I make my home.
9. I believe that a shift in consciousness, rather than advances in technologies, is the principal means to overcoming our planetary crisis.
10. I attend to the wisdom of deserts, forests, oceans and rivers, mountains, and grasslands as I continue to learn that to be wholly human is to be wild.

Imagine that you and I have joined together with a community of people dedicated to reclaiming their wild souls. It is a warm summer evening, and our bare feet touch the soft ground as the setting sun lights the tips of the grasses like candles. We link hands and form a circle.

We are gently and yet firmly enveloped and enfolded in the curving embrace of our Earthly home. Listen to the rustle of the wind, breathe the wild air, sense the salty oceans swirling in your veins; feel how the Earth evokes an answering response in your own wild soul.

May all the blessings of the Earth be yours. And may all of yours be shared with her.

Additional Resources

Many writers and poets have influenced my own thinking, imagination, and writing and I owe a debt of gratitude to each of them. The following is just a sampling, but it is a rich one. It has much to offer the wild soul.

Introduction to the Soulscapes
Books and Essays

Abram, David. *The Spell of the Sensuous*, Vintage Books, New York, 1996. Abram's lyrical and expressive writing reevaluates our place in the world, arguing that human cognition is dependent on the natural world. Many of his stories have shifted my consciousness about the relationship between language and landscape. One told of the time he sought refuge from a storm in a mossy cave, only to see the galaxies written in rain-sparkled spider webs.

Berry, Thomas. *The Dream of the Earth*, Sierra Club Books, San Francisco, 1988. Also: *The Universe Story* (with Brian Swimme), HarperSanFrancisco, San Francisco, 1992; *The Great Work: Our Way into the Future*, Bell Tower, New York, 1999. A cultural historian, Berry has mentored me through his writings. The books listed have been particular sources of inspiration, providing a brilliant framework for reenvisioning the realms of ethics, politics, economics, and education in the light of cosmology and ecology. His broad scope and deep intellect provide a moral vision to light my path forward.

Estés, Clarissa Pinkola. W*omen Who Run with the Wolves: Myths and Stories of the Wild Woman Archetype*, Ballantine Books, New York, 1992. This book revived and reanimated my love of wildness through mythic storytelling. Pinkola Estés's writing is lush, poetic, and rooted in the wild feminine. A therapist trained in Jungian psychology, she is a powerful source of wild archetypes.

Griffin, Susan. *Woman and Nature: The Roaring Inside Her*. Harper & Row, New York, 1978. Griffin combines philosophy, science, myth, and history, weaves in wild and poetic prose, and creates a book that breaks down boundaries at every turn. In reading it, I came not only to see but also to feel how closely women are identified with the Earth—as both life givers and victims of rage.

Roszak, Theodore. *Voice of the Earth: An Exploration of Ecopsychology*, Phanes Press, Inc., Grand Rapids, Michigan, 2001. A professor of history, Roszak questions the divide between psychology and ecology. He writes, "Once upon a time all psychologies were 'ecopsychologies.'" Addressing the limitations of a modern therapeutic model that denies and ignores our connection to the Earth, he reveals that the wounds of the Earth are our wounds as well.

Snyder, Gary. *The Practice of the Wild*, North Point Press, San Francisco, 1990. In his brilliant opening essay, "The Etiquette of Freedom," Snyder writes that the word "wild" is usually defined in terms of what it is not: civilized, obedient, manageable. This book, however, gives us a sense of what "wild" is. His wide-roaming essays offer a vivid articulation of what freedom, wildness, goodness, and grace mean. Where Snyder goes, I follow.

Thoreau, Henry David. "Walking," Cosimo Classics, New York, 2006 (first published 1862). This is the quintessential nature essay. It begins with a manifesto: "I wish to speak a word for Nature, for absolute freedom and wildness, as contrasted with a freedom and culture merely civil." Thoreau is so advanced—or ancient—in his thinking that he feels like a modern-day ecologist. We all walk in his footsteps.

Poetry

Harjo, Joy. "Remember," in *She Had Some Horses*, Thunder's Mouth Press, New York, 1983, 1997. Harjo's drumbeat repetition of the word "remember," used fifteen times in this one poem, calls us back to our true selves. We only need to remember we are one with the world of wind, animals, plants, ancestors, and stars. This poem speaks to me about who we truly are and of what we are truly made.

DVDs

Swimme, Brian. *The Powers of the Universe*, DVD series, 2005. (http://www.story-oftheuniverse.org). Swimme was my husband's mentor at the California Institute of Integral Studies. We were fortunate to be present for the filming of this series, which presents a new understanding of the cosmological principles coursing through each of us. Swimme inspires me to live my life in a larger way, aligned with the great evolving story of the Universe.

Publications

Orion Magazine came out in 1982. Its first editor in chief defined the magazine's values this way: "It is *Orion*'s fundamental conviction that humans are morally responsible for the world in which we live, and that the individual comes to sense this responsibility as he or she develops a personal bond with nature." *Orion* is one of the few magazines my husband and I still receive in print. Rebecca Solnit, Barry Lopez, Derrick Jensen, David Abram, and many other environmental writers (and artists and photographers) find a platform for their powerful messages in these pages, and I've discovered many of my favorite writers here. www.orionmagazine.org.

Deserts

Books

Bruce Chatwin. *The Songlines*, Penguin Books, New York, 1988. The aborigines of Australia believe their totem ancestors sang the world to life. In Chatwin's lively travelogue, the theme is one of becoming deeply intimate with the land by walking across it and continually mapping our path with "dreaming tracks" or "songlines." In the songlines I found my own map to a deeper appreciation and knowledge of the world about me.

Thomas, Elizabeth Marshall. *The Old Ways: A Story of the First People,* Farrar, Straus and Giroux, New York, 2006 A vivid account of her family's time spent living with the Bushmen of the Kalahari, in which the author provides insight into a people considered the closest relatives to our original ancestors who arose out of Africa. I listened to this as an audio book while camping in the Mojave Desert's Death Valley. A stunning portrait of an ancient people, it allowed me a glimpse into the origins of a more primal and Earth-aware self.

Reisner, Marc. *Cadillac Desert: The American West and Its Disappearing Water,* revised edition, Penguin Books, New York, 1986, 1993. A devastating account of our careless and grandiose attitude toward the desert and the precious water that sustains it. To read this brilliant and absorbing book is to understand the limitations and dangers of technology as well as the underlying hubris that fuels grand schemes that have little to do with the reality of ecosystems. If the desert is a place of mirages, it is our own human illusions that are proving the most dangerous ones.

Williams, Terry Tempest. *Refuge: An Unnatural History of Family and Place,* Vintage Books, New York, 2001. Also *Red: Passion and Patience in the Desert,* Vintage Books, New York, 2002. In a single paragraph in her memoir *Refuge,* Terry Tempest Williams repeats the phrase "I believe in . . ." three times to describe her faith in the ability of deserts to teach us—about humility, mutual dependency, the spirits that have moved on. Every visit to the desert is "a pilgrimage to the self." In *Red,* whether dedicating a whole chapter to listing the names of red-rock wilderness areas or expounding on Aldo Leopold, she is fighting for the preservation of these neglected places. Of Leopold she writes, "I can honestly say it is Aldo Leopold's voice I continue to hear whenever I put pen to paper in the name of wildness." In writing of the desert, it is Terry Tempest Williams's voice that whispers to me.

Poetry

Wagoner, David. "The Silence of the Stars," *Traveling Light: Collected and New Poems*, University of Illinois Press, Urbana, 1999. The poet takes the subject of his poem from a story told by the South African writer Laurens van der Post about his time spent living with the Bushmen of the Kalahari. Wagoner contrasts the Bushmen's limited material possessions with their rich connection to the sacred cosmos. The poem invites this question: are the advances of modern civilization compensation for our present-day deafness to the natural world?

Forests

Books

Hill, Julia Butterfly. *Legacy of Luna: The Story of a Tree, a Woman, and the Struggle to Save the Redwoods*, HarperSanFrancisco, San Francisco, 2000. This book, and Maathai's below, are examples of trees awakening a sense of love and protection for the natural world, and that just one person can make a difference. *Legacy of Luna* is a firsthand account of Hill's two years spent living in a 180-foot, thousand-year-old grandmother redwood tree in Humboldt County, California. In her heroic quest to save the ancient tree from the chainsaw, Butterfly Hill recalls the women of the Chipko movement of India, who protest deforestation and save the forests by placing their bodies between the trees and the chainsaws.

Jensen, Derrick, and George Draffan. *Strangely Like War: The Global Assault on Forests*, Chelsea Green Publishing, White Junction, Vermont, 2003. Likening the bloodthirsty approach of deforestation to the savagery of war, this book brings home the depths of the horror that accompanies our brutal approach to clear-cutting forests. Difficult and heartbreaking to read at times, it links the viable future of humanity to our ability to protect the planet's dwindling forests. It forced me to confront our aggressiveness toward the Earth.

Maathai, Wangari. *Unbowed: A Memoir*, Anchor Books, New York, 2007. Nobel Peace Prize winner Wangari Maathai offers her account of her childhood in rural Kenya and her emergence as founder of the Green Belt Movement. Like Hill's memoir, her book speaks of ways in which planting trees can inspire radical change.

O'Donohue, John. *Anam Cara: A Book of Celtic Wisdom*, HarperCollins, London,1997. O'Donohue explores the relationship between darkness and light that is at the heart of the forest soulscape and of the Celtic tradition from which he emerges. He writes, "Each thing creeps back into its own nature within the shelter of the dark." In language that is lyrical and lush, he shows me that the soul is shy, and needs some measure of darkness to thrive.

Poetry

Wagoner, David. "Lost," *Traveling Light: Collected Poems*, Indiana University Press, Bloomington, 1999. The poem begins with a command: "Stand still." This is good advice for those of us lost in the forest. In twelve short lines, the poet conveys the tension we experience when off track and off trail. Wagoner's poem suggests that rather than running, we root ourselves in the present moment and take in the place of "Here." I have used this poem many, many times in my poetry groups, and I always make new discoveries.

Lawrence, D. H. "Escape," *The Complete Poems of D. H. Lawrence*, Wordsworth Edition, Ware, UK, 1994. Lawrence grew up on a farm at the edge of the woods. Perhaps that's why he understands the wild, liberating nature of the forest so well. His poem inspires in me an animal joy, a sense of pure exhilaration. Escaping into the forest with Lawrence, I reconnect with a primal sense of power.

De Boer, Lauren. "Earth Said." http://terravitabooks.net. My friend and colleague Lauren de Boer has kindly granted me permission to share the following poem, which has often accompanied me on my forest walks. You can learn more about his work and writings at his website.

Earth Said

Be like a tree. Stay rooted in the dream
that breathed you here.
Give yourself fully to the seasons,
let change be change,
a strong full wind
that quickens the sky
from dark to light, and back.
Let the storms come and pass.
There is a time to leaf and flower,
A time to release and be dormant.

A tree doesn't worry or fret
about whether it is an oak or a bay laurel,
a sycamore or an elm;
about whether the bend of branch
or the coiffure of canopy is in fashion.
It gives itself to being alive.

A tree doesn't know success or failure;
they don't exist
in the mind of bark and branch,
are only concepts
in a mind that's forgotten.
Be like a tree. Hold your limbs upward
to beseech the sky.

Oceans and Rivers
Books and Essays

House, Freeman. *Totem Salmon: Life Lesson from Another Species*, Beacon Press, Boston, 1999. In his account of restoring the native salmon runs in the Mattole River Valley of Northern California, the author captures the magnificence of the salmon's journey from river to ocean and back again to the mother river. Reading this lyrical and vivid story of return, I felt the importance of restoring wildness to streams—and to souls. House reminds us that each creature has the right to his own habitat and wild, ancient way of life.

Pielou, E. C. *Fresh Water*, University of Chicago Press, Chicago, 1998. This book delivers the science of water with passion and poetry, covering the history, state, and future of fresh water. Pielou's particular genius is in providing novel ways to look at water. She compares a watershed, for example, with a remote indigenous tribe—both are self-contained, finely honed communities, perfectly adapted to their environments. If that isolation is destroyed, both fall apart.

Ehrlich, Gretel. "The Source of a River," in *Islands, the Universe, Home*, Penguin Books, New York, 1992. Out of this stunning range of essays on the relationship between humans and the natural world, I find myself returning most often to this piece. Ehrlich's ability to seamlessly flow from inner to outer landscape is extraordinary. In her search for the source of the Yellowstone River, she concludes, "To trace the history of a river or a raindrop, as John Muir would have done, is also to trace the history of the soul . . ." Indeed, it is.

Poetry

Hogan, Linda. "Journey," in *Rounding the Human Corners*, Coffee House Press, Minneapolis, 2008. How would it be to live like the river, as if everything lay before us? There is a primal, pulsing energy to this poem. Reading it is like riding a wild river—or a wild horse—or just a great and gorgeous current of wildness.

Oliver, Mary. "The Sea," in *House of Light*, Beacon Press, Boston, 1990. Stroke by stroke, the poet invites us to reimagine our beginnings as creatures of the oceans, with fins and gills and scaled bodies. We have forgotten our origins, but Oliver's poem returns us to our psychic and physical beginnings as creatures of the deep. After reading this poem, I dreamed I could breathe underwater.

David Whyte, "The Sea," in *Where Many Rivers Meet*, Many Rivers Press, Langley, WA, 1990. This poem takes as its focus the ocean's drawing tide. Beneath our surface worries about money and success, there is a greater current at work, Whyte tells us. The poem invited me to imagine what it would be like to tap into the flow of my true longing.

Mountains
Books and Essays

La Chapelle, Dolores. *Earth Wisdom*, Guild of Tutors Press, Los Angeles, 1978. Most of Earth's major religions began in a visionary experience on a sacred mountain. This book explores the power of the rocky earth to shape our thinking and bring us closer to the divine. Our mind, as deep ecologist La Chappelle reminds us, is not limited to the space within the human skull, but is embedded in the whole of nature.

Leopold, Aldo. *Sand County Almanac: With Essays on Conservation from Round River*, Oxford University Press, New York, 1949. What if the mountain doesn't want us to kill the wolf? Only the mountain has lived long enough to know what is good for the mountain and what is not. Leopold's deep insight into the interconnectedness of life—and the trophic cascade effect—came to be known as "thinking like a mountain."

Muir, John. "A Near View of the High Sierra," in *Nature Writings*, The Library of America, New York, 1997. In this collection of essays, Muir captures his fascination with and love of the Sierra Nevada mountain range. He shares with us a sense of delight at the great expansiveness and sense of freedom he experienced in the mountains. Muir suffered from depression, yet the mountains lifted him into ecstasy.

Poetry

Ignatow, David. "The Explorer," in *New and Collected Poems, 1970–1985*, Wesleyan University Press, Middletown CT, 1986. To some, the risk taken in climbing a mountain can appear unnecessary. But what if the mountain is ours to climb?

Doesn't that change everything? This deceptively simple poem helped me understand the difference between climbing for a dream that serves my soul and reaching for one that doesn't.

Grasslands
Books and Essays

Eiseley, Loren. "How Flowers Changed the World," in *The Immense Journey: An Imaginative Naturalist Explores the Mysteries of Man and Nature*, Random House, New York, 1957. Every essay in this collection is extraordinary: lyrical, brilliant, scientific. This essay, however, changed me. I came to realize that flowers and fruits enabled us to store the kind of energy that would grow our brains and evolve our species. Writes Eiseley, "The weight of a petal has changed the face of the world and made it ours."

Harwell, Karen, and Joanna Reynolds, *Exploring a Sense of Place: How to Create Your Own Local Program for Reconnecting with Nature*, Conexions: Partnership for a Sustainable Future, Palo Alto, CA, 2006. Writes farmer and poet Wendell Berry, "You can't know who you are until you know where you are." This book seeks to address this truth by offering engaging exercises to help us become intimate with the bioregion in which we live.

Manning, Richard. *Grassland: The History, Biology, Politics, and Promise of the American Prairie*, Penguin Books, New York, 1995. How does America's relationship with the grasslands reflect our relationship to nature, ourselves, and the way we see the world? Manning mourns the loss of the prairies as he reimagines their restoration as a means of reclaiming a vital link to our own prehistoric roots. This book helped me see how battling the prairies and battling the forces of evil got so strangely and disastrously entwined.

Poetry

Berry, Wendell. "In a Country Once Forested," in *Given: Poems*, Counterpoint Press, Berkeley, 2005. The "farmer poet" and novelist/essayist Berry's works promote an essential message: we must learn to live in harmony with the natural rhythms of the earth or perish. In this poem he invites us to remember, ". . . under the pavement the soil / is dreaming of grass."

Oliver, Mary. "The Summer Day," in *New and Selected Poems*, Beacon Press, Boston, 1992. The sweet smell of summer and grasses and long idle days are perfectly captured in this much-quoted poem by Mary Oliver. She invites us to savor life, and teaches me that every moment is precious and blessed.

Robinson, Ann. "What the Earth Denies Us." Robinson is a poet, friend, and sometime farmer. This poem perfectly reveals the heartbreak of those who are so intimate with the land that they recognize the damage being done to it. Her forthcoming book of poetry, *Stone Window*, is due out 2014. This poem is used with her permission.

What the Earth Denies Us

My worst nightmare is to tell you
I wake up and there is no rain,
days, weeks;
the fields pour heat. My wells, dry.
Mornings I blame God for lack of groundwater,
not the big boys at Monsanto
who give us Roundup beans, herbicides,
synthetic hearts and cells,
but God who hides behind dry clouds,
and only watches.
You would not recognize me, God,
a damp shirttail, boots clinging
to sand and hope.
A woman who owns her own farm and doesn't pay bills.
My farmhands drive broken down combines,
smoking, watch the earth sour in the hot wind.
Hoping a woman fails, but still wanting a job.
A snake crawled on my boot
on row 43 and died.
My corn a cracked lair.
Bollweevils in cotton.
This is my farm, my irrigation ditches.
A woman understands why the birds no longer gather,
the seasons shift beyond recognition.
I look out my window on the evening,
The ghosts of cattle egrets float across the moon,
the stars fold on each other
and lose memory.
I am thin now. These crops were our masonry.
And still I pray.

Walking the Wild Edge
Books

Lake, Osprey Orielle, *Uprising for the Earth: Reconnecting Culture with Nature*, White Cloud Press, Ashland, 2010. As a renowned sculptor and committed activist for social and environmental justice, Lake brings a unique perspective to the intersection between the manmade and the wild. In her wise and poetic book, she explores an Earth etiquette that recognizes the rights of both human communities and more-than-human communities. She has an understanding of what it will take to successfully walk the "Wild Edge."

Acknowledgments

The writing of this book has taken almost a decade, and during those years there have been many times when I found myself lost in the forest, unable to find my way forward. I was fortunate, however, to have many brilliant and generous people shine their light along the path so I could eventually find my way home. This is my inadequate attempt to thank them all.

First and foremost, my gratitude goes to Kathy Kuser. Her earth-based coaching model, cocreated with Virginia Kellogg, set the stage for what would later evolve—through my collaboration with Kathy—into an early version of the soulscapes. This book owes much to her formative thinking and her wise and wild spirit.

Kay Adams, founder of the Center for Journal Therapy and a cherished friend and mentor, encouraged me to develop my wild soul work as I trained with her to become a facilitator of poetry therapy. She was also one of a group of early readers that included my husband, Bruce Thompson; Kate Thompson (no relation); William (Bill) Carney, and Lauren de Boer. They championed me, challenged me, and inspired me in ways both small and significant.

Wendy Wallbridge, a sister on the writing path, offered encouragement and smart suggestions over the years. Brooke Warner helped me establish an inviting balance between the personal and the planetary at a crucial time in the book's evolution. Hannelore Hahn gave me the gift of believing in me both as a writing teacher and a writer. Rachel de Baere, Jeffrey Erkelens, and Marilyn Steele have contributed to this work as well.

This book would have never come about without the support of my weekly writing group. The ever-insightful feedback of Ann Robinson, Lee Doyle, and Julia McNeal encouraged me to rewrite until I got it right. My fondest memory: Lee's finger moving to the penultimate passage of a rough draft as she said, "I really like how it reads from here on down, Mary!"

My heartfelt thanks go to Peter Barnes for giving me my first taste of unadulterated writing time as a resident of Mesa Refuge in Point Reyes Station in West Marin County. I'd still be trying to finish this book if it weren't for Peter's generosity. To my Mesa Refuge cohorts, Jane Juska and Mary Nelen, goes my fondest appreciation for creating a home away from home for two weeks. My debt to Jane is especially acute. She nudged me with her round-heeled shoes and showed me I was trying to control the soulscapes by writing tidy chapters of equal length for each. Jane was never one to like conformity.

Students, clients, and friends shared their wild stories and responses to the landscape generously with me in workshops and classes, and over walks and cups of coffee. I am so grateful to them for aiding me in the discovery of Earth's archetypes.

Linda Gelbrich, Susan Field, Kristin Reynolds, Cyncie Winters, Caroline Brumleve, Katie Diepenbrock, Lonner Holden, Mary Jo Ott, and Don Moseman have candidly shared their stories. There are those, too, who chose to remain anonymous but still gifted me with their insights and experiences. Most particularly, my thanks go to all my students at the Therapeutic Writing Institute; introducing the soulscapes to them was a profound experience that supported me in keeping my faith and focus.

If writers are lucky, they have great editors. I am one lucky writer. Julia McNeal and Sheridan McCarthy have my deepest respect and gratitude for their love and command of the written word. They are among a select few who understand how much depends, among other things, on the precise placement of a comma. Richard Riddle, Amanda Tomlin, and Stanton Nelson saved my sanity by helping with endnotes, permissions, and other devilish details.

Thanks to Steve Scholl and White Cloud Press for publishing the first edition of this book. As well, to Christy Collins of Constellation Book Services for your superb book design—thank you!

Sophie Brudenell-Bruce created the powerful images that so perfectly capture the mythic and archetypal nature of the landscapes. Sophie and I have been friends since we met at the Convent of the Holy Child in Cavendish Square in London at age five. I am so grateful that she chose to develop her talent for art, which was evident even at an early age, and that she so generously brought it to bear upon this project. Lorraine Anderson's beautiful foreword has also blessed this book. Her own books, many of them anthologies dedicated to women's nature writings, bless us all.

Finally, in the human world, my greatest thanks go to my husband, Bruce Thompson. He has read many versions of this book and shared his wisdom unstintingly throughout. As a graduate student earning his masters in philosophy, cosmology, and consciousness from the California Institute of Integral Studies, he introduced me to the works of Brian Swimme, Thomas Berry, Mary Evelyn Tucker, Linda Hogan, Susan Griffin, and many other authors and thinkers who have influenced this book. Bruce continues to share his wisdom with me as adjunct professor at CIIS, teaching ecological economics. He is brilliant, kind, and patient beyond reason. He adds, "Don't forget phenomenally handsome too." I love him deeply and forever.

On many days, finding myself stuck, I laced up my hiking boots and headed outdoors. Surrounded by trees, sky, meadows—Mount Tamalpais beckoning in the distance—the answers came. It is to the Earth that this book, and my deepest gratitude, truly belong.

Notes

Preface

1. Clarice Short, "The Old One and the Wind," in Lorraine Anderson, ed., *Sisters of the Earth: Women's Prose and Poetry About Nature*. New York: Vintage, 2003, 152–53.

Introduction

1. Thomas Berry, *The Dream of the Earth*. San Francisco: Sierra Club, 2006, 195.
2. Gary Snyder, *The Practice of the Wild*. San Francisco: North Point, 1990, 101.

Chapter 1

1. Max Picard, *The World of Silence*. Stanley Godman, tr. Chicago: Regnery, 1952, 19.

Chapter 6

1. Georgia O'Keeffe, "About myself" in Georgia O'Keeffe: Exhibition of Oils and Pastels. New York: An American Place; 1939.

Part 2: Forests

1. Dante Alighieri, *The Divine Comedy: Inferno*. John Aitken Carlyle, tr. London: Chapman and Hall, 1849, 2.
2. Gerard Manley Hopkins, "The Blessed Virgin Compared to the Air we Breathe," in *Poems of Gerard Manley Hopkins*. Robert Bridges, ed. London: Humphrey Milford, 1918, 45.
3. Henry David Thoreau, *Walden*, Radford, VA: Wilder Publications, 2008, 107.

Chapter 8

1. Jerry Mander, *In the Absence of the Sacred*. San Francisco: Sierra Club, 1991, 257–59.

Chapter 9

1. Eve Ensler, *Insecure at Last: A Political Memoir*. New York: Villard, 2008, xx.

Chapter 11

1. David Suzuki and Wayne Grady, *Tree: A Life Story*. Vancouver and Berkeley: Greystone, 2004, 3.
2. Willa Cather, *O Pioneers!* Boston and New York: Houghton Mifflin, 1913, Part II, Chapter XIII, 153.

Chapter 12

1. T. S. Eliot, *The Use of Poetry and the Use of Criticism*. Cambridge, MA: Harvard University Press, 1932, 144.

2. Rainer Maria Rilke, *Letters to a Young Poet*. Stephen Mitchell, tr. New York: Vintage; 1984, 23.

Part 3: Oceans and Rivers

1. David Whyte, "Sweet Darkness," in *The House of Belonging*. Langley, WA: Many Rivers, 1997, 23. Reprinted with the permission of Many Rivers Press.

Chapter 14

1. Thomas Merton, *The Wisdom of the Desert*. New York: New Directions, 1970, 11.

Chapter 16

1. Inspired by a writing prompt given by Eunice Scarfe based on the poem by Di Brandt, "Prairie Love Song," in Agnes in the Sky. Winnipeg, Manitoba: Turnstone Press, 1990.

2. Langston Hughes, "The Negro Speaks of Rivers," in *The Collected Poems of Langston Hughes*. New York: Knopf, 1994, 23. Reprinted with permission of Random House.

Chapter 19

1. C. G. Jung, Visions: Notes of the Seminar Given in 1930-1934. Ed. by Claire Douglas. Princeton University Press, 1997, 333–34.

Chapter 20

1. Ocean Robbins blog, posted May 14, 2011. http://oceanrobbins.com/blog/

2. I heard Huston Smith say this during a talk.

Chapter 21

1. John (Fire) Lame Deer and Richard Erdoes, *Lame Deer: Seeker of Visions*. New York: Simon and Schuster, 1972, 113.

2. Carl G. Jung, *Memories, Dreams, Reflections*. New York: Vintage Books, 1965, 223.

Chapter 22

1. Rainer Maria Rilke "In Widening Circles," in *Rilke's Book of Hours: Love Poems to God*. Anita Barrows and Joanna Macy, tr. and ed. New York: Riverhead, 1997, 45. Reprinted with permission of Riverhead Books, an imprint of Penguin Group (USA) Inc.

Chapter 23
1. Aldo Leopold, *A Sand County Almanac: And Sketches from Here and There*. New York: Oxford University Press, 1949, 129–32.

Chapter 24
1. Linnie Marsh Wolfe, *John of the Mountains: The Unpublished Journals of John Muir*. Madison, WI: University of Wisconsin Press, 1938, 296.

Chapter 25
1. John Muir, *The Mountains of California*. New York: Penguin, 1997, 44–45.

Chapter 27
1. Li Po, "Zazen on Ching-t'ing Mountain," in *Crossing the Yellow River: Three Hundred Poems from the Chinese*. Sam Hamill, tr. Rochester, NY: BOA Editions, Ltd., 2000, 94. Reprinted with permission.

Chapter 28
1. Terry Tempest Williams, *Finding Beauty in a Broken World*. New York: Vintage, 2009, 190.
2. William Faulkner, The Art of Fiction No. 12" (Interviewed by Jean Stein). *Paris Review*, Spring 1956.

Chapter 32
1. Carolyn Griffin, October 9, 2008 blog by Gary Hardwick: http://www.norman-transcript.com/religion/x519029095/God-is-beauty/print.
2. Wendell Berry, "In a Country Once Forested," in *Given: Poems*. Berkeley: Counterpoint, 2006, 345. Reprinted with permission of Counterpoint.

Chapter 33
1. Robert Frost, "Mending Wall," in *Poems by Robert Frost: A Boy's Will and North of Boston*, New York: Signet Classic, 2001, 678.
2. Cited in Stevanne Auerbach, *Confronting the Child Care Crisis*. Boston: Beacon, 1979.
3. Rilke, "Too Alone," in *Rilke's Book of Hours: Love Poems to God*. Anita Barrows and Joanna Macy, tr. and ed. New York: Riverhead, 1997, 67. Reprinted with permission of Riverhead Books, an imprint of Penguin Group (USA) Inc.

About the Author

Mary Reynolds Thompson is a facilitator of poetry and journal therapy and life coach dedicated to bringing forth the Wild Soul Story. This new story is rooted in our oneness with nature and a vision of a world in which the wild landscapes of both Earth and soul can thrive. Her own connection to the sacred Earth has been key to her thirty-year recovery from alcoholism and grounds her in an understanding of how we can all awaken from the addictive trance of the modern world. She is also author of *Embrace Your Inner Wild: 52 Reflections for an Eco-Centric World* (White Cloud Press, 2011), as well as numerous essays on eco-spirituality. Core faculty for the Therapeutic Writing Institute and founder of Write the Damn Book, she conducts writing and eco-spirituality workshops and retreats throughout the world. Born and raised in London, England, today she lives in her beloved landscape of Marin County, California, with her husband, Bruce. www.maryreynoldsthompson.com

About the Artist

Sophie Brudenell-Bruce is a painter and printmaker working and exhibiting in London and France. After twelve years as a garden designer, Sophie returned to full-time painting in 1992. The human figure remains central to her work, but exploration of other media, in particular printmaking, has given her the freedom to investigate the realms of controlled abstraction. She is married with four children. Sophie can be contacted through her website, www.sophiebb.com.

Made in the USA
Middletown, DE
16 June 2023

32712880R00106